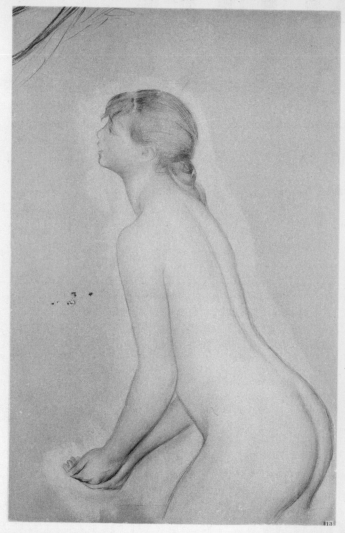

AUGUSTE RENOIR   **BAIGNEUSE**

APPLES AND MADONNAS

EMOTIONAL EXPRESSION IN MODERN ART

BY C · J · BULLIET

NEW REVISED AND ENLARGED EDITION

NEW YORK
COVICI · FRIEDE · PUBLISHERS

Instead of a FOREWORD

EXPRESSIONISM *has long outgrown the stage in
which it called forth only the horrified shrieks of the
old fogies and the moral indignation of the "great ones"
dominating the art world. There are plenty of Philistines yet, it is true, who consider that when they
have applied the epithets "hideous, barbaric, clumsy,
perverse, pathological" to the new tendencies in art,
they have done their duty as artists and as citizens.
But even these narrow-minded devotees must find food
for reflection in the fact that the representatives of the
alleged horrible and inartistic productions have also
achieved very important things in traditional art, and
have often devoted themselves with truly religious*

[v]

seriousness and with a sense of awe to this entirely un-orthodox movement. It will be a further source of uneasiness to these same narrow-minded persons that in the most diverse spheres of culture the same spirit which revolts against traditional standards and impetuously pours out new works of art is making itself felt in painting, sculpture, architecture, poetry, music.

—DR. OSKAR PFISTER in *"Expressionism in Art."*

CONTENTS

CONTENTS

ILLUSTRATIONS

[ix]

ILLUSTRATIONS

ILLUSTRATIONS

APPLES
AND MADONNAS

OF
APPLES
AND
MADONNAS

An apple by Paul Cézanne is of more consequence artistically than the head of a Madonna by Raphael.

In the development we know as "Modernism"— which is the reaffirmation and emphasizing of a strain that has been in art since the first caveman carved by the light of flaming faggots the reindeer and the mammoth of the hunt — it is the emotional power of the artist that counts, not the subject matter.

Paul Cézanne, highest god of the new Pantheon, is one of the few supremely great souls of all time.

Glancing back through the ages, into which he himself is slowly retiring, we encounter, of his stature, only Rembrandt, El Greco, Michelangelo and Giotto. These

[3]

are souls of great driving force — souls that expressed themselves in form and color with the sledge-hammer genius of a Shakespeare and an Ibsen in drama — a Beethoven in music.

Just what genius is, has not been clearly defined, despite the herculean labors of the psychologists and the scientists. But its manifestations are unmistakably sensed. A Rembrandt has a vigorous vitality that a Van Dyck just falls short of; Shakespeare has a life force that Marlowe just missed; Beethoven throbs with blood a little redder than Mozart's.

Cézanne's apples, expressed with an elemental force akin to the forces of nature — crude and rugged — that bring apples into being, are superior to the heads of Raphael's Madonnas — piquant Italian girls, transferred almost literally to the canvas with the adroit skill of the master draftsman of all time, but without emotional travail. It takes an El Greco Virgin to match a Cézanne apple.

Cézanne is the one supreme pattern of "Modernism".

"The primitive of the way", he modestly regarded himself, but it is a way nobody has succeeded in blazing any further. Followers along the trail, encountering certain marks of the giant, have ventured off into side paths ——

"Nature can be expressed by the cube, the cone, and the cylinder", he once observed. "Anyone who can

[4]

paint these simple forms can paint Nature", and off into the jungle wandered the Cubists.

Cézanne, classed in the early days of the Paris art revolution with the Impressionists, is the focus of "Modernism". He is not only its supreme figure, but its logical center. The rebellion, started against the authority of Napoleon's pseudo-Roman David, culminated in Cézanne; and since Cézanne, everything of consequence that has happened reverts back to him.

Cézanne's nurture was the technique of Impressionism, that amazing manifestation of Naturalism, whose devotees sought to catch exactly the appearance of a tree, or a house, or a haystack at some particular moment of sunlight or shadow. In their eagerness for the delicate surface appearance of things, they forgot form — a fundamental in art from the birth of time.

"I wish to make of Impressionism something solid and enduring like the art of the Old Masters", said Cézanne, and he attained his ambition. In reasserting form, he did not lose the very valuable contribution the Impressionists had made to painting — luminosity.

Cézanne, then, is a logical development and not the violent anarchist of art his enemies have sought to make him appear. He is a revolutionist — perhaps the greatest in art of all time — but he did not spring, like a twin of the warrior Athene, full-fledged from the forehead of Jove. He had worthy antecedents — as had

Shakespeare — and worthy contemporaries, and worthy disciples, all a part of a great art movement, in which he holds leadership by the unassailable power of superior genius.

A short history of

MODERNISM

through the ages

"MODERN ART" is 14,000 years old by the lowest calculations acceptable outside of Genesis-ridden Tennessee. How much older, it is impossible to say, since the work of possible Matisses and Picassos who flourished before the skilled draftsmen of 12,000 B. C. is lost.

In caves of Spain, France and Austria are still to be seen scratched on the walls highly "Modernistic" drawings by reindeer hunters who flourished in the Quaternary Period that came to an end about 120 centuries before the Christian era. These are pictures of deer, bison, wolves and the mammoth, executed with the sensitive feeling for line that only an Aubrey Beardsley or a Henri Matisse has exhibited in our own time.

Swinging now into the ken of the Fundamentalists, we may observe that all Egyptian art is "Modern", including the Cubistic Sphinx (possibly Ethiopian in its origin).

All Chinese art from the remotest antiquity to the present day is "Modern".

All Japanese art, except what has been produced in the last fifty years under Occidental influences, is "Modern".

All Greek sculpture before the Fifth Century B. C. is "Modern".

All Persian art of characteristic pattern is "Modern"— and all Hindoo art, and all African art.

Art that is not "Modern" had its origin in Greece about the time of Pericles, and reached the highest perfection it has ever known in the marbles of Praxiteles and possibly in the paintings of Apelles — though the greatest work of this painter and the one that survived longest fell into decay and ruin in the time of Nero — his Venus rising out of the waves — and there is no way to judge now except by hearsay. Cabanel possibly was not far wrong in his guess at the spirit of the Venus of Apelles when he did his famous "Birth of Venus", long an ornament of the Luxembourg — and of a million souvenir post cards.

After the "golden age" of Greece, the art that is not "Modern" gradually gave way again to "Modernism", which reigned supreme during the Dark Ages — especially in the astonishing Byzantine period — until the Italian Renaissance.

PABLO PICASSO   PORTRAIT OF A MAN

All this is roughly accurate — this present sketch aiming, for the time being, only at a rapid general survey, without going into technical details and without noting technical exceptions.

It's about time, at this point, to define "Modernism"— and here again the definition will be only rough and non-technical.

"Modernism", be it noted first, however, is not "crudity", as its enemies insist. The Primitives back even to the reindeer hunters were often highly skilled; and the world has never seen more adroit draftsmen than the Chinese and the Persians.

"Modernism" has to do with "mood". The "Modernist" creates by inner impulsion and not by slavish copying of his model — person, object or landscape. He aims at emotional effect without consideration of photographic accuracy — though photographic accuracy is not excluded necessarily — sometimes it is used with most astounding results.

Aside from technical considerations, that is about all there is to "Modernism".

The art opposed to "Modernism" is the art that has developed — and to a very high degree of technical perfection — through application of rules.

Aside from the very vital fact that rules always deaden spontaneous creation, this art, guided by the schools, aimed at exact reproduction of the model — aimed, and had all but attained its object, when the camera stepped in, and, according to the "Modernists", destroyed forever the usefulness of mere imitative art — the camera, they assert, can do the work much better than the hand, and with much greater rapidity.

Academic art, it must be observed in fairness, does not always aim at camera-like perfection, any more than "Modern Art" avoids scrupulously the exact appearance of things.

Art becomes "academic" when it submits to formula — when the individual spirit of the artist dies. The "Academic", as we know it today, may be said to have originated with the Carracci in Italy, who reduced Raphael, the great popular hero of the Renaissance, to formula, and peopled Europe with a swarm of minor Raphaels — to the irreparable injury of the painter of the Sistine Madonna.

Revolts have been numerous since — one of the rebels, Caravaggio, making a violent noise even in the days of the Carracci themselves — but it was not until our own time that the rebels threw off definitely the yoke that had been clamped by the enterprising Italian schoolmasters about the neck of art.

Courbet fired the first giant cannon in the successful revolution with his Manifesto of 1855, backed by his painting, "The Funeral at Ornans"; and the battle has been carried on to complete victory by succeeding generals — Edouard Manet, Claude Monet, Paul Cézanne, Henri Matisse, Pablo Picasso.

It is the tendency of the "Academy", once a rebel victory is won, to reduce the victor to formula, and thus start a new phase of "Academism". That was what happened to the rebel art of Claude Monet — his "Impressionism", done by rule, is now the "Academic" art of England and America, whose practitioners scoff at the smooth nudes of Bouguereau and Cabanel, leaders of the "Academy" in the days of the Monet revolt.

In Continental Europe, similarly, the art of Paul Cézanne, which followed "Impressionism", has been formulated, and is becoming "Academic".

All the world over, the sculpture of Rodin has become the type toward which the armies of sculptors without genius aspire.

This does not mean that Monet, Cézanne and Rodin cease to be great emotional masters — great "Modernists". But it does mean that their legions of mediocre disciples, not animated by the original impulse, are merely "Academic" and of no consequence.

Even so bizarre an art development as "Cubism" has its "academic" fringe. In certain of the studios of Paris, "Cubism" was taught for a time to all aspirants toward fantastic extremes of "Modernism"— students capable only of surface imitation. Picasso doesn't suffer in the tastes of those who know, but the world has been flooded with bad "Cubism", just as it has been flooded with bad "Impressionism".

Though "Modernism" lay practically dormant in

Europe for nearly 400 years under the iron sway of the Carracci and their successors, its fires were never quite quenched, and burst forth only into a hotter flame that developed into a holocaust with the fanning by Courbet and his followers.

To the picturesque Italian vagabond and murderer, Caravaggio, belongs the credit of lighting the taper of revolt.

The Carracci, a Bolognese family of painters, brothers and cousins, all of them highly talented, and one, Annibale, of decided genius, founded an academy in 1585. For the purpose of instruction, they reduced to formula the marble statues of the "Golden Age" of Greece, and performed the same doubtful service for Correggio and Raphael. The mill of the Carracci — a highly efficient machine — soon was turning out hosts of painters and sculptors, working by rule — all of about even merit.

The restless Caravaggio, of Rome and Naples — wherever the authorities would allow him to light — a born revolutionist who would have disturbed the world at any period into which he had happened to be born — led a revolt against the Carracci. He gathered around him a few followers, and the rivalry of the "Independents" and the "School" became so keen and so personal that resort was had to sword and dagger, and minor pitched battles were fought. (So belligerent was Caravaggio, that when there were no enemies to fight, he

was apt to turn on his friends and disciples — Guido
Reni, for one.)

Among Caravaggio's followers was the Spaniard
Ribera, and through Ribera the spirit of independence
was carried into Spain, where already was at work the
man of mystery, the Cretan El Greco. The Carracci
won out in Italy, and their art by formula became domi-
nant through Europe — the art extracted from Raphael
combined with the art distilled from the Greek classic
marbles. This art persisted officially until the triumph of
Impressionism, about the beginning of the present
century.

In obscure, unimportant Spain, the spirit of Caravaggio "carried on". The young Velasquez had caught
the contagion from Ribera. The rebel fires of El Greco
and Velasquez, smouldering for nearly two centuries,
burst out afresh in the flashing Goya.

Courbet was not insensitive to the Spanish influence
— El Greco and Velasquez were among his idols — but
it was from Goya that Edouard Manet lit his torch of
revolution — parent of the flame that swept the entire
art world.

Aside from Paul Cézanne, Edouard Manet is the
most important figure in the "Modern" movement.
Courbet had forged the thunderbolt, but Manet
launched it, and then, like a god of Homer, rushed himself into the punctured citadel of the enemy, followed
by his rabble of rebels, and completed the devastation.

Manet forced onto a reluctant world an uncompromising Realism. Nymphs and Arcadian shepherds were driven out of the woodlands they had so long inhabited — the harlot "Olympia" supplanted the coy Venus.

Events moved swiftly. For a time, the star of Manet was dimmed by a spectacular new star that arose beside it — the star of Claude Monet — but, as in the physical heavens, when the stella nova faded (in our own day), the star of Manet resumed its brilliance.

Claude Monet became the chief developer of the new "Impressionism", which Manet had originated. He pushed it to an extreme of tenuosity as thin as the tail of a comet. When it was noted that nothing lay beyond Monet's "Impressionism", just as nothing lies beyond the Venus de Milo, there came the counter revolution, led by Paul Cézanne. Edouard Manet was dead.

Cézanne abandoned the surface aspect of things — which had been the ultimate aim and end of Monet — and began searching for structural profundity. The search led back to the very fork in the road where Monet had diverged from Manet — back to Goya — back to Rubens and El Greco — back to Chardin and Poussin — back to Rembrandt — back to the Byzantines — back to the Greek Primitives, and the Chinese and the Egyptians — "Modernists" all, whatever their date in the Gregorian calendar.

Simultaneously with Cézanne, there arose those other two giants of the pioneer days of "Modernism"—

Paul Gauguin and Vincent Van Gogh, more spontaneous in their origin than Cézanne himself, whose evolution is no mystery — but not of his stature.

Another figure appeared, too, Georges Seurat, inventor of Pointillism, growing out of Impressionism — on a different stem from Cézanne's. Seurat, because of the high artificiality of his method, was abandoned with more or less contempt by the eager followers of Cézanne in the first flush of Post-Impressionism. But he has since been assigned to a rightful place among the giants — a lone giant, the sole exponent of a method wrong in its philosophy, but of such individual genius that he is spectacularly triumphant.

Beside Cézanne, too, stands his former comrade in Impressionism, Auguste Renoir, who, like Cézanne and Seurat, abandoned the lead of Claude Monet, but also went his individual way — painting, finally, the most brilliant female nudes in the entire history of art through the ages.

Of the period of Cézanne, too, is that queer genius, Henri Rousseau, the douanier, scarcely "all there" in his head — developing from nowhere, unless out of the "subconscious" of Art — the most original manifestation in the whole "Modernist" movement — a "freak", and yet strangely powerful as a painter.

After Cézanne came a host of eager investigators, who ransacked all art of all times for "inspiration".

Matisse found it in Persian art, principally, and in the art of the Hindoos, and in Fra Fillippo Lippi.

Picasso found it in Negro sculpture, and in the Moorish geometrics of the Alhambra and his native Andalusia, and in El Greco, and in Piero della Francesca and in Botticelli.

These, in turn, have inspired a younger group — though Picasso is still only in his forties, and Matisse is not yet sixty.

Marie Laurencin, for example, caught something from Picasso's "Blue Period"— something that filtered through from Botticelli — and developed it into the most orginal and delicately feminine art the world has ever known. And Andre Lhote has attempted the astonishing feat of reconciling Picasso's "Cubism" with the "Classicism" of Napoleon's pet David — and all but succeeded.

EL GRECO　　　　　　　　　　　　　　　ST. MARTIN

Thrilling Adventures Among
THE "ISMS"

BEFORE plunging into the maelstrom of the "isms", it might be well to focus some terms, especially since they have been loosely applied and with varying meanings by competent authorities, and ignorantly misconstrued by "critics" and museum lecturers, who are at sea generally about everything that has developed in art since Claude Monet.

The invention of the term "Post-Impressionism" is credited to Roger Fry who, in 1910, spread it as a sort of blanket over all the art reactions from "Impressionism". The term covered Cézanne, Van Gogh and Gauguin, the trio of original rebels, besides Matisse and his *"Fauves"* of Paris and Picasso and his brood of "Cubists". "Post-Impressionism" was as broad in its application as "Impressionism" had originally been — "Impressionism", which had embraced almost polar types — Degas and Monet.

"Post-Impressionism" is not particularly satisfactory. It is merely chronological — the art that came after "Impressionism"— and connotes nothing of the aims of the new men. A better term was applied to the German "Post-Impressionists"— namely "Expressionists". The "Expressionists", in the strict application of the word as first used, were extreme "Post-Impressionists", allied with the French "Cubists" and the Italian "Futurists", but the term has since been made looser in its application in Germany, and has been given a still wider territory, confined no longer to the German movement.

"Expressionism" is not more satisfactory in describing the aims of "Modernism" than "Impressionism" had been in defining rigidly what was going on in Paris art circles in the 1870's. But it is the best term that has been suggested to give a general idea of the aims of the new men.

"Expressionism" suggests that the artists it labels are seeking to "express" their individual reactions toward their models. All artists of all ages worthy of the name have done that, just as all great artists, and not alone the "Impressionists", have sought to give an "impression" of the object being painted. But the "Expressionists" have insisted on their point of subjective reaction, letting the external impression of things take care of itself. "Expressionism" will be used in these discussions very often in this wider application.

Between "Impressionism" and "Post-Impressionism" there was a short period of "Neo-Impressionism"
— that is to say, "Impressionism" that had become
highly sophisticated — too scientific, dry of emotionalism. "Neo-Impressionism" reached its climax in "Pointillism". The "Impressionists" had laid colors side by side
in such a way as to blend, at a certain distance, in the
eye of the beholder, so as to give the effect of light and
not merely of color. The "Pointillists" sought to achieve
the effect by little dots or "points" of color. The leading
exponents of the method were Seurat, Signac and, for
a period, Pissarro, who had been chief co-worker with
Claude Monet in developing to its farthest limits the
practice of "Impressionism". "Pointillism" was short-
lived, but during its brief span it gave to the world
Seurat, a painter of superior genius — a great artist,
despite the high artificiality of his method, just as Alexander Pope was a great poet.

"Post-Impressionism" was not long in developing
smaller, well-defined groups.

The German "Expressionists", with their unconcern
over the natural appearance of things — an unconcern
that would have worried Cézanne — have carried distortion to a point of torturous agony undreamed of in
the wildest delirium of Blake or the somber fits of the
religious mysticism of El Greco.

In France arose "Cubism", with its bizarre angles
and planes thrown apparently helter-skelter into a can-

vas at the unrestrained whim of the painter. This "mad" aspect, however, slowly passed as it began to be realized that the genuine artists working in the method were in earnest, seeking abstract designs of beauty comparable with the patterns of the Arabs and the Persians; and "Cubism", at first the joke even of the artists, developed into the most salutary movement in all the manifestations of "Modernism". It clarified the murky atmosphere as even Cézanne could not have done without its aid. It was the chlorine the waters of art needed — waters made impure through the ages by the dumping of the sewage of the Academies. "Cubism" was defined by its foremost literary spokesman, Apollinaire, as being "not an art of imitation but a conception that tends to rise itself as a creation."

From Parisian "Cubism", there developed in Italy "Futurism." "Cubism," especially in its greatest master Picasso, is more or less static. It takes from its model lines and planes and lays them onto the canvas, not in a naturalistic order, but in an order that fits into the created design of the painter.

"Futurism," however, according to its chief spokesman, Boccioni, "abolished quietness and statism and demonstrated movement, dynamism. It has documented the new conception of space by confronting the interior and the exterior. For us, gesture will not any more be a fixed moment in universal dynamism: it will be the dynamic sensation eternalized as such."

The aims of "Futurism", shorn of the mysticism with which the makers of art manifestos — like prophets of religion — love to envelop their movements, seem to include the expression in a single design, not only of the internal and external features of the model, but also the appearance of today and yesterday and tomorrow. In other words, the "Futurists" introduced a time element into "Cubism"— the "fourth dimension" of space, as mystical philosophers among the mathematicians insist. It was this time element that was supposed to galvanize "Cubism" into life.

"Futurism", in its original manifestation in Italy, resulted in little of consequence — nothing at all comparable with the best canvases of Picasso and Leger among the "Cubists"— but there is a current revival of interest in the movement, from which the artists hope great things.

In England, "Cubism" also had a child, yclept "Vorticism". Its parentage has been ascribed, too, to "Futurism", in which case "Cubism" would be its grandfather. It's a wise art child that can distinguish its grandfather from its father.

"Vorticism" was even more futile than "Futurism" — probably because its only genius, the sculptor Gaudier-Brzeska, was killed, a very young man, in the World War, before he could give "Vorticism" any definite tendency. Those who "carried on", especially the painter Wyndham Lewis, spoke vaguely of "spiritual weight", and under this "weight" was crushed "Vor-ticism".

"Dadaism" is the climax of the folly of the "Isms" — when the artists began to manufacture them in a spirit of satire and sport.

"Dadaism has carried affirmation and negation up to nonsense", wrote one of its most able exponents, Arp. "In order to come to indifference, Dadaism was de-structive."

"Dadaism", according to Arp, "gave the clyster to Venus of Milo and allowed Laocoon & Sons to absent themselves at last after they had tortured themselves in the millennial fight with the rattlesnakes."

Even "Dadaism" has a youngster, "Merzism". "All that the artist spits is art", according to the "Dadaist", Kurt Schwitters, its sponsor.

"Constructivism" has been making a noise in Russia, Holland and Germany, and has been found of great practical utility in the designing of stage settings — the most important of all the "Modern" develop-ments in this field.

"Constructivism," officially, "proves that the limits between mathematics and art, between a work of art and a technical invention, are not to be fixed."

Some interesting things have been done in the method in both pure painting and sculpture, in addition to stage settings; and the Bauhaus experimental school at Weimar, where the movement at present is largely focused, is one of the live spots of the art world.

All "Modern Art" has more or less of the "abstract" in it, but some of the frenzied extremists have raised the abstract to the dignity of an "ism". Giving form to the inobjective they call "Abstractivism".

The woods, a decade ago, were full of other "Isms", most of which died of inanition.

There was "Suprematism", for example, that declared "the midnight of art is ringing", and so reduced all painting to a black square on a white canvas.

"Purism" aimed to produce "precise physiological sensations in the spectator" by means of abstract lines and geometrical designs.

"Neoplasticism" spoke mystically of dividing the rectangle "horizontally-vertically" so as to obtain "tranquillity, the balance of the duality".

"Verism" proved in the hands of Georg Grosz, its German advocate — most powerful of living satirists — as good as its definition: "to hold the mirror before the grimaces of the artist's contemporaries." Grosz was "spoofing"— more of him anon.

There arose, also, a school of "Metaphysicians" in art, aiming to "represent the immaterial by the material" and "happy to use museums as asylums for old age."

"Simultanism", perhaps a "woods colt" of "Futurism", had to do with color and color contrasts in the expression of "representative movement."

"Compressionism" was a sort of substantial, three-dimensional "Cubism".

Even the motion picture film was on the road to development of a special "ism"— a development recently resumed in this country (imported from the Germans), tending toward a new abstraction.

It is curious to note the tyranny exercised by a name in these art movements. When you christen your baby boy Algernon or Percy, you are apt to do him an irreparable injury — though there have been some valiant souls that have overcome the suggestion. Many a sweet high school girl has been wrecked by having her companions nickname her Tommy or Billy. So it is with art movements. Let some satirist hit upon a name for what was originally a spontaneous manifestation of genius, and its whole course is apt to be altered.

Take "Cubism" for example. When Henri Matisse, a *Fauve* who happened to be obsessed by gracefully curved lines, dubbed, in a spirit of ironic fun, the severely mathematical compositions of his friends Braque and Picasso *Cubisme*, he started the process of congealing a fluid art as surely as a December wind starts congealing the waters of a creek. The cylinder and the cone belonged as much to the theory of Picasso — working on the suggestion of Cézanne — as did the cube. But the term "Cubism" decided the destiny of the move-

J. B. S. CHARDIN

ment. Braque and Picasso themselves seem to have felt the iron sway of the name, and all their followers, with the exception of Leger, were unable to resist the suggestion. "Cubistic" art became largely a matter of "cubes."

Similarly with "Impressionism". Claude Monet and his associates were interested primarily in the problem of illuminating their canvas — so manipulating colors, that is, that they would give the effect of light, not mere brilliance and gaudiness. The Little Dutch Masters had made some progress in this direction, and so had Claude Lorrain, and so, emphatically, had the Englishman Turner, whose dazzling snow was a direct inspiration to the French impulse. Monet and Pissarro, consciously and keenly, set to work developing on canvas a scientific theory they had devised from the studies of Helmholtz in his analysis of light.

In 1874, Monet exhibited, with thirty other of his despised and ridiculed associates, in a photographer's gallery. It was the first extensive display of the "idiotic" new canvases. One of Monet's canvases was entitled "Sunrise — An Impression". Louis Leroy, critic of the Paris Charivari, headlined his article of satiric denunciation: "Exposition of the Impressionists". The name stuck. The members of the *Société Anonyme* (their official designation) rather liked the new name themselves, just as a little band of Romans nineteen centuries ago found something attractive, even though it was hissed and howled, in the epithet "Christian".

"Impressions" they began to paint, through sheer suggestion of the name. Even Claude Monet was intrigued. Had the witty M. Leroy written a different headline for his comic article in Charivari, April 25, 1874, the chances are our "Waterloo Bridges" would be less evanescent.

Another and very modern instance is "Vorticism."

"Vorticism" primarily, it seems, had to do with color. It was interested in a mystical something called "spiritual weight"— the soul of things. This "spiritual weight", it would appear, could be expressed only in "primary pigment". There was a sort of intensive center of spirituality into which ideas are constantly, irresistibly rushing — a "vortex".

The "vortex", in this original conception, was no more a physical, visible vortex than the blending of colors so as to produce light was an "impression". But the term "vortex" was so highly suggestive of a point toward which lines converge that the "Vorticists" started making "vortex" drawings — which they are doing even unto this day, having lost sight of the "spiritual weight" of their original manifestos. The "Vorticists" originally, like the "Futurists", were sworn foes of the "Cubists". Today, with their mathematical vortices, they are only a minor tribe in the realm of "Cubism".

"Dadaism", which deserves to be spanked, is still another case in point. *Dada* is, in French, a "hobbyhorse". The original idea of "Dadaism" seems to have been to throw off all restraint. Let anybody mount his hobby-horse and ride helter-skelter. Let no artist feel himself bound by the reigning "Post-Impressionism" in France, the reigning "Expressionism" in Germany, the reigning "Impressionism" in England and the United States.

It wasn't necessary for the artist, however, to consider his hobby-horse a bull and dash into a china shop. He could gallop off in the direction of Raphael and Michelangelo, if he wanted to. But "Dada" has another significance, understandable in many languages, including the Flapperese — the infantile cry of "Daddy!"

The "Dadaists" began babbling foolishly like a baby or a chorus girl. And "Dadaism", as a serious art movement, collapsed before it got started.

OF EDOUARD MANET
and the Rumbles of Revolution

HAD Edouard Manet not listened to the siren voice of his friend, Claude Monet, the era of Post-Impressionism and Paul Cézanne might have dawned a score of years earlier. But then the world would have missed the lovely rainbow mirage of Impressionism.

Manet was the stronger character — Monet the more enthusiastic dreamer.

Edouard Manet, having sat at the feet of Courbet and having made an immortal journey to Spain and beheld the wonders of Goya, was inspired with a new vision of Naturalism.

He paraphrased Giorgione's "Concert" in the Louvre into "Lunch on the Grass"; he gazed on the lovely sleeping Venus of the same Italian master, and — remembering, too, Goya's nude "Maja" — painted the harlot "Olympia"; miles and miles of religious paintings in the Louvre and the Prado fanned the fire in his rebel blood, and he painted "Jesus Insulted by the Soldiers".

Howls of derision and execration arose from the Paris mobs that swarmed excitedly before these pictures when he dared exhibit them. The police were called in to guard his canvases from the knives of fanatics.

Manet became the hero of all the young artists disdainful of the Academy, with its iron grooves of method and its deadly discipline — young Claude Monet among them.

In the midst of the excitement, Monet displayed some of his work in a shop window. Manet heard about it and was annoyed — evidently a young upstart, taking a name similar to his, playing on his reputation.

Manet, a little later, repented of his hasty judgment. This Monet, he saw, was driving at something quite different — different and original. He was attempting to put light into his canvases, instead of just color.

Manet not only observed and understood, but grew enthusiastic. Instead of master, he became disciple — to his detriment. For Manet had not the sensitive eye of Monet for subtle tones in light and color. Neither he nor anyone else ever matched the painter of the twenty haystacks and the fifteen Waterloo bridges in fleeting evanescence of surface beauty.

The Impressionism of Claude Monet — its only supreme master — diverted Edouard Manet from the straight course of his original, rugged naturalistic genius. It gave his work a certain delightful buoyancy, but it robbed it of strength that might have been his in approximate measure with Cézanne's.

For in Cézanne, to the very last, are traces of his first spectacular hero, the revolutionist Manet, whose battles with the Salon and with the police stirred his own enthusiasm. Manet's strength, as exhibited in his early work, at times challenges Cézanne's own. Manet died in 1883 without reaching his highest possible destiny.

The rebellion of Edouard Manet against the official Salon of Paris back in the Sixties, leading to the order of Napoleon III to establish the *Salon des Refusés*, is the most spectacular if not the most important art event in the history of the world.

Revolt had long been in the air. It may have been an outgrowth of the spirit that engendered the French Revolution.

The French Revolution, like the Russian Revolution of our own day, was followed at first by an iron-heeled tyranny more repressive of intellectual and emotional independence than that from which the revolution had freed the minds of men. There is a certain parallel in our own battle to make the world safe for democracy, saddling us with irksome repressions America had not experienced since the years immediately preceding 1776.

In the case of Paris, Louis David was the particular wet blanket Napoleon Bonaparte laid heavily on Art. Napoleon inherited David from the Royal regime — Napoleon, despite the boast that he was his own ancestor, was a social climber of a type so obvious as to be visited by the scorn and contempt which those in the social swim always mete out to aspirants — even though as in his case they tremble at his name. David, with his Graeco-Roman inspiration, was already a celebrity before the fall of the Bastille. In his "Oath of the Tennis Court", he demonstrated he knew how to trim his sails to the winds of revolution, and he proved his Imperialism in "The Coronation of Napoleon in Notre Dame."

Despite his political shiftings, which probably meant as little to him as the politic admiration for George Washington meant to the Tory Gilbert Stuart, David remained firm to his neo-Classic ideals. He was a powerful painter, despite his severe imitation of the bas-reliefs of Greece and Rome — so powerful, indeed, that certain of our very recent "Modernists" are beginning to hark back to him. His was a driving personality, too, and backed by the favor of the Emperor, he dominated almost unquestioned the art of Paris, then as now the art capital of the world.

Almost unquestioned, but not quite. Prud'hon, David's most formidable rival, was an admirer of the earlier Greek beauty, and produced sensuous pictures, in contrast with the Graeco-Roman iron of David. This quality, scorned by David, who referred to Prud'hon as another Boucher, became important in the revolt against the authority of Napoleon's favorite. The rebellion started in earnest in the Salon of 1819, with Gericault's "Raft of the Medusa"— the first pot-shot of the Romantics. Three years later, Delacroix, emulating Gericault, exhibited "Virgil and Dante in the Inferno".

David's well-wishers tried to stem the current setting strong against the authority of the master by launching the work of David's brilliant pupil, Ingres.

The choice was an unfortunate one, however, for Ingres had, like Prud'hon, much of the Greek in his art blood, with a generous number of the corpuscles of Raphael. The ideals of David went glimmering, and the battle developed into a fight for supremacy between Ingres, a better artist than his master, and Delacroix — Gericault, meanwhile, having died.

Chasseriau, pumping the blood of Romanticism into the forms of the Classicists, might have reconciled the warring schools, had not other factors been injected into the fight. The Fontainebleau school was rising, with its fresh vision of nature — a sort of romantic realism — Rousseau, Dupré, Daubigny, Millet. Corot had made his advent with his dreamy forest trees.

All of these painters were seeing life ecstatically through the tinted glasses of some form or other of Classic tradition, when suddenly the gruff, violent voice of Gustave Courbet was heard.

EDOUARD MANET

Courbet, originally a disciple of Prud'hon, had come latterly under the influence of Velasquez, and then, through a native genius of his own, had undertaken to paint things as they are. In 1855, he published his Manifesto, setting forth his ideas of a rational Naturalism — father of a legion of Manifestos that have infested the art world since.

Courbet backed up his Manifesto with such naturalistic things as "Funeral at Ornans" and *Bonjour, Monsieur Courbet* — tame and "academic" enough now, but so fiery and revolutionary in their own day that Courbet is even yet remembered vaguely as a low and vulgar fellow.

In the turmoil of excitement that attended Courbet's revolt against an anemic Classicism in all its forms, the even more spectacular Edouard Manet appeared, and since 1863, when "Lunch on the Grass" was rejected by the official Salon and Napoleon III inaugurated the *Salon des Refusés*, the art world has not known a moment's peace.

Manet was only one of a number of restless rebels following in the footsteps of Courbet — good enough to exhibit in the rather liberal Salon, but viewed askance — when the members of the Institute, the Salon jury, made the most unfortunate slip in the history of Academism and rejected Manet's paraphrase of Giorgione's "Concert". The Emperor was appealed to in behalf of Manet and certain other youngsters rejected, and ordered a gallery set aside for them in the same Palace of Industry where the official show was to be held, in order that the public might judge between the Institute and the rebels. "Lunch on the Grass," displayed along with paintings by Whistler, Fantin-Latour, Bracquemont, Cals, Chintreuil, Harpignies, Laurens, Legros, Pissarro, Vallon and others, was by far the most spectacular picture in the Salon of the Rejected, and upon it centered the storm of indignation.

In the picture are four human figures in a woodland spot, two men and two women. One of the women is completely nude, and the other partially so, while the two men are fully clothed.

The picture was condemned as frightfully immoral — in vain Manet and his friends pointed to Giorgione's *Le Concert Champêtre* in the Louvre, only a few blocks away, where exactly the same idea had been used — contrasting the white flesh of the women against the dark clothing of the men.

As late as 1925, an American sculptor and writer, F. W. Ruckstull, discussing this picture, poured on it a vitriol that may be regarded as a concentrated distillate of the moral indignation it has excited in certain breasts for three-quarters of a century.

"The picture explains itself," says Ruckstull, in his big volume of desperately savage vilification of all that is "Modern", entitled "Great Works of Art".

"Two couples, evidently free lovers, have rowed in

a boat to a sylvan spot in a forest. While the two women bathe in the stream and disport themselves nakedly before these men, they look on and afterwards have their lunch. And, while one of the men pretends to talk, two others of the party are represented as if posing for their portraits, the woman particularly being self-conscious in her look. Moreover, she is plain to coarseness.

"If a good citizen should happen to run onto such a scene suddenly, by mistake, he would be shocked stiff."

Good citizens, by the same token, should fight shy of all rooms where Greek sculpture is displayed, should be careful never to visit the Vatican, with its murals by Michelangelo — and, when in the Louvre, should always be ready to turn their backs on a goodly percentage of the Old Masters — as one of our Chicago female art "critics" confesses proudly she did in front of "Olympia".

Manet, at once, with "Lunch on the Grass"— which was called in that first showing "The Bath" — sprang into the limelight, and until his death twenty years later the spot was never off him. He seems to have revelled in the sensationalism that attended his every move, but certain of his friends have declared the first blaze of publicity, with its savage indignation, was too violent even for his tough courage.

In 1863, the year of his sudden advent into notoriety, he painted "Olympia". This was the year, too, of his marriage with the daughter of the Dutch sculptor, Leenhoff. He did not venture to exhibit this picture until 1865, and then only at the urgent importunities of his wife.

The "Olympia" scandal was even more sensational than that of 1863. The police had to be called in to protect the canvas from the knives of enraged art fanatics. The painting was roped off, so nobody could get near it, but even that didn't protect it from being spit on.

Another of Manet's paintings, hung in the same exhibition, "Jesus Insulted by the Soldiers"— now in the Art Institute of Chicago — had to be similarly protected. "Jesus Insulted" appears innocent and tame enough now — in comparison, say, with Gauguin's "Yellow Christ" and Marc Chagall's grinning Figure on the Cross — and it is almost incredible it should have aroused such wrath when first shown, and in liberal Paris. Christ was a human being, grimy and suffering, instead of the idealized figure of the stained glass windows in a thousand churches — just as "Olympia" was a human harlot, instead of the idealized wanton Giorgione depicted and called Venus.

"Olympia" remained a scandal throughout Manet's life — and, indeed, for a score of years after his death — arousing indignation whenever shown. However, when "Olympia" was about to go to America, she was purchased for the French government by subscription raised by Claude Monet. And, a few years later, Georges Clemenceau, a life-long friend of Manet's, literally forced her into the Louvre, when he was in power — to the perpetual scandal, perhaps, of maiden lady "art critics" touring the Louvre in search of culture.

"Olympia" is a reclining nude — not unlike, in composition, the sleeping Venus of Giorgione and the waking Venus of his disciple Titian — resembling, too, Goya's nude "Maja", hid for years in royal cellars. Manet "sinned" in not idealizing her —"Olympia" is a *fille de joie*, naked and unashamed.

A very human Magdalene in the Paris of 1865 was insulted and spat upon, along with a very human Christ.

Manet was the individual sensation of those early days of the revolution, but by 1874 the "heresy", of which he was the central figure, had come so definitely into the consciousness of Paris that the town was ready to accept Louis Leroy's designation of the group, "Impressionists"— derived from Monet's painting, *Impression: Soleil Levant.*

Among the exhibitors that memorable year — and the year preceding — were Pissarro, Monet, Sisley, Renoir, Berthe Morisot, Cézanne, Degas and Guillaumin, besides a score of lesser lights, such as Brandon, Boudin, Cals, Collin, Labouche, Bracquemont, Lepine and Rouart, little more now than names. Manet did not exhibit regularly with his friends, but he was classed with them, and looked upon as their leader.

Little distinction was made by the critics among the two score recognized "Impressionists" — lumped together into a common mess for contempt — though two extremes were vaguely indicated — Manet, almost within the bounds of respectability, and Cézanne, winner without question of the booby prize. How different it all appears now, in the light of later developments, with the atmosphere clarified, and in the perspective the years always create.

Only Claude Monet and Pissarro traveled the entire way Impressionism was destined to go, with Sisley limping along after them. Monet attained the sublime heights, with Pissarro just a step or two down the slope. Monet fixed light on canvas — light in distinction from color — as no mortal ever had done before, or probably ever will do again. He was the supreme flower of "Impressionism".

Cézanne gave up definitely and decisively the quest for the rainbow of surface loveliness, and devoted his genius to solidity underneath surface appearances. He became the leader of the counter-revolution — the Post-Impressionist general who put to rout the hosts of his friend and former master, the gentle Pissarro, faithful lieutenant of Claude Monet.

Renoir, who had a richer, more barbaric color — flashing like jewels — than any of his fellows, when they were all striving to break up color and resolve it into light, abandoned, too, the quest for the elusive, tenuous rainbow. His colors gave a quality of warm sensuousness even to his landscapes — unlike the coolness of the landscapes of Monet.

Renoir chose to develop his colors instead of breaking them up, and became the supreme master of the female nude.

Manet progressed only a little way along the path he saw his friend Monet going — he died before Monet had made the entire journey. By his side traveled his faithful pupil, sister-in-law and female reflection, Berthe Morisot — always a Manet in petticoats, though she had a very real talent and was not a mere copyist. Her inspiration, rather, developed along with his. After the death of Manet, Berthe Morisot continued a while to paint, but made no further progress.

Faithful, too, to Manet was Mary Cassatt, the American, erstwhile pupil of Degas. She lived past four score, dying in 1926, preceding Claude Monet only a few months to the grave. But Mary Cassatt, like Berthe Morisot, never developed beyond the Manet who died in 1883.

Degas, the other genius of the 1874 show, was never an Impressionist at all — even when "Impressionism" was a broad enough term to cover both Monet and Manet.

Degas, who found a marvelous sisterly relationship to exist between washerwomen and ballet girls, is of another line of descent which has contributed handsomely to "Modernism" without being of the immediate family. He is akin to two other giants — great serious painters, with, however, a savage strain of satire that approaches caricature — Daumier and Toulouse-Lautrec.

Daumier, a newspaper cartoonist and illustrator, was taken seriously as a painter only by a few friends like Corot, who might well sympathize with him. For Corot, imprisoned in his own forest of highly marketable trees, was painting for his own satisfaction a series of powerful female nudes, which he turned to the wall for fear a sight of them might injure the sale of his trees. These nudes may yet place Corot high in the rank of "Modernists". Corot tried to interest Paris in the powerful figures Daumier was doing in paint about the same time the "Impressionists" were making their noise, but couldn't be heard in the din.

Daumier was a great "Modernist" before the star of Cézanne arose. After him came Degas and then Toulouse-Lautrec — greater than Degas, though lesser than Daumier — and the line is continued somewhat feebly in Forain.

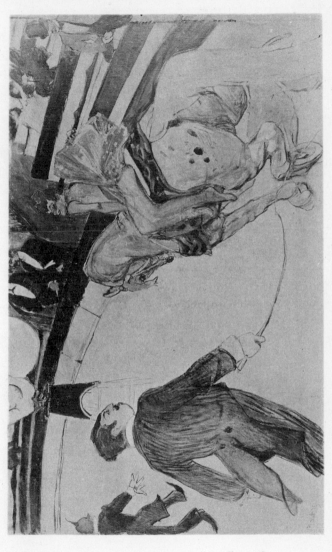

TOULOUSE-LAUTREC

OF PAUL CÉZANNE
the Hermit Rebel

EMILE ZOLA, literary champion of the Paris rebels of the 1870's, died in 1902, believing the chum of his youth, Paul Cézanne, a failure.

Practically all of Cézanne's work was spread out before Zola, for the painter was to follow the novelist to the grave only four years later. And yet Zola, who had sensed Manet back in the days of the *Salon des Refusés*, was unable to grasp the significance of a greater master, at his elbow.

It may be the human brain is capable of only one great revolutionary thrill. The veteran painters living today whose youthful enthusiasm was aroused by Claude Monet are cold to the message of Pablo Picasso. The sculptors who shivered with delight when Rodin was defying the lightning of the gods of the Academy refuse to respond to the rebel shouts of Archipenko.

James Huneker, easily the best critic of the arts

America has produced, was, like Zola, numb to the genius of Cézanne. In "Promenades of an Impressionist", four years after the death of the master of Aix, he writes of a visit to the Salle Cézanne, reverently incorporated in the Autumn Salon:

"Sacred ground, indeed, we trod as we gazed and wondered before these crude, violent, sincere, ugly, bizarre canvases. Here was the very hub of the Independents' universe. Here the results of a hard-laboring painter, without taste, without the faculty of selection, without vision, culture — one is tempted to add, intellect — who with dogged persistency has painted in the face of mockery, painted portraits, landscapes, flowers, houses, figures, painted everything, painted himself. And what paint! Stubborn, with an instinctive hatred of academic poses, of the atmosphere of the studio, of the hired model, of 'literary', or of mere digital cleverness. Cézanne has dropped out of his scheme harmony, melody, beauty — classic, romantic, symbolic, what you will! — and doggedly represented the ugliness of things."

Huneker, who had discovered for America Claude Monet, and Richard Wagner and Henrik Ibsen, was still so dazzled by the fairyland surface loveliness of Impressionism that he saw only as ugliness and discord the rugged beauties, the powerful harmonies of Cézanne.

Strange it is today to read Cézanne was "without taste", in the presence of *"L'Estaque"*; "without the faculty of selection", when gazing at his "Card Players"; "without vision", with that miraculous composition of "Bathers" in the forest before you; "without culture", in the charmed atmosphere of any one of his infinitely delicate water colors; "without intellect", confronted by any one of his self-portraits. "Harmony, melody, beauty", instead of being "dropped out of his scheme" are recaptured from Rembrandt, Chardin and El Greco and restored to painting after the lapse of centuries.

Huneker had a sub-conscious perception, however, for he adds:

"But there is a brutal tang of the soil that is bitter, and also strangely invigorating, after the false, perfumed boudoir art of so many of his contemporaries."

Huneker, however, like Zola, died without sensing the significance of the giant of "Modernism". For in his last utterance — in "Steeplejack", of date 1918 — twelve years after the death of Cézanne, and when all the young painters of Europe had bowed to the terrific authority of the master, Huneker could still observe:

"The chiefest misconception of Cézanne is that of the theoretical fanatics who not only proclaim him *chef d'ecole* — which he is — but also declare him to be the greatest painter that wielded a brush since the Byzantines. The nervous, shrinking man I saw years ago at Aix-la-Provence would have been astounded if he had known that he would be saluted with such uncritical rhapsodies."

Maybe — and maybe not.

Much has been made by both friends and foes of Cézanne's "inferiority complex"— of his oft-repeated plaint that he was "unable to realize"— of his self-effacing assertion that he was only "the primitive of the way" he had discovered. He was saying these things only a year before his death.

But what do you make of his other utterances, as set out by Ambroise Vollard in his sparkling biography?

"All my compatriots are asses compared with me", Cézanne writes to his son Paul, Oct. 15, 1906, seven days before he died from a cold caught painting in a field in a storm. "I think the younger painters are much more intelligent than the others; to the old ones I am just a disastrous rival."

Discussing his break with Zola, who had insulted him, he believed, by sketching his portrait in the sensational novel *l'Oeuvre,* Cézanne told Vollard:

"You can't ask a man to talk sensibly about the art of painting if he simply doesn't know anything about it. But by God!"— and here, Vollard relates, Cézanne began to tap on the table like a deaf man — "how can he dare to say that a painter is done for because he has painted one bad picture? When a picture isn't realized, you pitch it in the fire and start another one!"

One day somebody bumped into him while he was at work in a field. "Don't you know that I'm Cézanne?" he shouted furiously.

"His friends bantered him a great deal about his obstinate determination to get into the official Salons; but we must not forget his conviction that, if ever he could slip into the Salon of Bouguereau with a 'well-realized' canvas, the scales would fall from the eyes of the public, and they would desert Bouguereau to follow the great artist that he felt himself capable of becoming."

So much for the "nervous, shrinking man" Huneker saw at Aix, "who would have been astounded if he had known that he would be saluted with such uncritical rhapsodies."

With a critic of Huneker's acumen missing so completely the point of Cézanne's genius, what wonder is it that the rank and file of newspaper "art critics" and museum lecturers should still be in the darkness, and Cézanne should still be looked upon as the Bloody Bones of art?

Cézanne had the fortune, bad or good, of being misunderstood from the start, even by his rebel associates and — especially cutting to his morbidly sensitive nature — by Emile Zola, of his native Aix, boyhood comrade and schoolmate.

Through the influence of Zola, whose literary talents developed early, and who became while still in his early twenties a distinguished newspaper writer and critic of the arts in Paris, Cézanne was received into the camp of the rebel painters, headed by Manet. So queer, however, was his art even in the realm where everything was queer, that his associates viewed him askance.

All the rebels — Manet, Monet, Pissarro, Berthe Morisot, Renoir, Sisley, and the rest — were mercilessly ridiculed by the public and by the critics, with the exception of their champion Zola.

But Cézanne had the misfortune to inspire distrust of his talents in his comrades, too. Zola gave him the cold shoulder — only slightly cool, perhaps, for Zola was of a kindly nature where his friends were concerned, however savage he was in fighting his foes — but cool enough for Cézanne to feel the chill.

Cézanne, in consequence, bitterly disappointed, deserted Paris, and became a hermit of his native Aix, where he worked out, in agony, his art salvation. Had he remained in the Latin Quarter, happy, he might never have struggled to "realize", but might have been content with the shallow honors of the Salon he sought and could have attained.

For twenty years he nursed resentment against Zola — but on hearing of the death of his old friend, he "wept and sobbed all day long."

Locked in Zola's cupboard were found the paintings Cézanne had presented him from time to time.

"I could never put them on the walls", Zola had told Vollard. "My house, you understand, is the rendezvous of artists. You know how fair-minded they are, yet severe with each other. I could not leave my best friend, the companion of my youth, to their tender mercies. Cézanne's pictures are under triple lock and key in a cupboard, safe from mischievous eyes. Do not ask me to get them out; it pains me so to think of what my friend might have been if he had only tried to direct his imagination and work out his form."

Renoir, only, in the early days seems to have had an inkling of what Cézanne was driving at — namely "to express form and light at the same time while sacrificing nothing whatever of local color", as his biographer Klingsor expresses it, or, in other words, to restore to painting the "form" it had in the days of Rembrandt, and Chardin, and El Greco, and Rubens, and Poussin (his gods), without sacrificing what the Impressionists had learned. Renoir, always a warm defender of Cézanne, profited by his example, generously acknowledging his indebtedness, and, like Cézanne, far outstripped their comrades, who remained faithful to the gospel of light.

Pissarro, without the same understanding, nevertheless was Cézanne's friend, also — Pissarro, the warm-hearted, generous Jew, least wordly wise of all the rebels, and most improvident of them in the matter of money — exploding an age-old fallacy regarding the blood of Shylock. It was through the patience of Pissarro in instructing him that Cézanne acquired enough of the new technique of Impressionism to lighten later the rugged strength of his form. They spent together a good part of the years 1872 and 1873.

Cézanne, from the first, followed an instinct for color that was peculiar to himself and that caused him to be distrusted even by the liberal-minded rebels of his comradeship. He drew by color instead of by line, which has given rise to the stupid theory, still held by "critics" and museum lecturers, that he could not draw. at all. He sought the exact tone of color, making it express volume and even perspective. Volume was a sort of obsession with. him — the eternal solidity of things, as opposed to the lovely surfaces of Claude Monet, whom, however, he passionately admired.

" 'Tis but an eye", he said of Monet, "but what an eye!"

In expressing volume with color tone, Cézanne quite often produced deformity of contour, which he would have avoided had he been a draftsman of line —"deformities" that no longer annoy, but that caused him to be reviled in his day by the jeering Parisians and to be viewed with suspicion by his friends.

It was in 1879 that Cézanne, who had been considering withdrawing from association with his com-

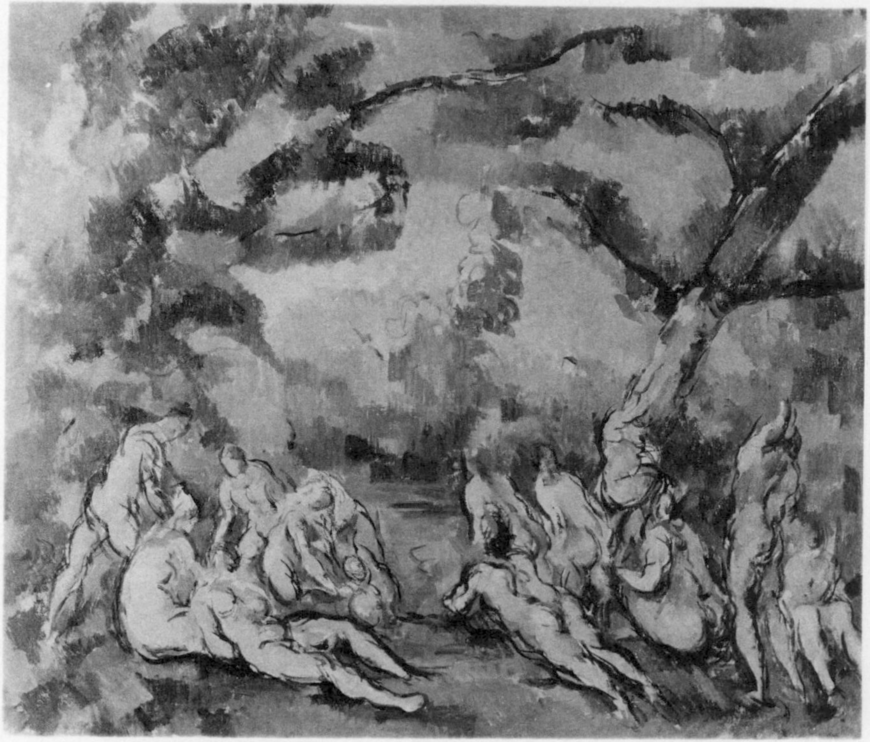

PAUL CEZANNE LES BAIGNEURS

rades since their first memorable exhibition in 1873, became so discouraged that he returned to Aix, there to remain the rest of his days, except for an occasional visit to Paris.

"He painted his near relatives, Madame Cézanne, or the neighbors, some old man or a farmer's son. And he became especially absorbed in the Aixoise country," relates Klingsor.

His neighbors, his relatives, even Mme. Cézanne, failed to understand him. "The affection of some one truly devoted to his art was denied him. If he had only had the happiness, like Rembrandt, to find a Hendrickje Stoffels! How much more valuable to an artist is a woman devoted to and confident of his genius, even though she be a servant, than a half enlightened pretentious person; of greater value a Hendrickje Stoffels than a fool like the Helene Surgeres who despised Ronsard. If the man, surrounded as he was by his mother, his sisters and his wife, benefited by their family affection, the artist in him was deprived of that affection, so much more ardent, more passionate and more admiring, which a woman (and only a woman) knows how to give. Cézanne could sympathize with him who envied Goya and the beautiful Duchess of Alba, who unveiled her lovely body before the painter. Not only was he deprived of such a model, but also of any being entirely moved by his painting."

Cézanne had not the luxuriant temperament of

Renoir, Rodin and Zorn that permitted them to surround themselves with nude female models. He was shy in the presence of women — so completely discomfitted if a pretty one undressed before him that he could not paint her at all. When he used a live female nude, she was either Mme. Cézanne or some woman so aged she no longer had powers that disturb.

In lieu of living models, Cézanne turned to Rubens. "He loved the ample modelling of the splendid nudes of the showy Flemish artist", relates Klingsor. "He would often pin on his wall a photograph of the group of Sirens in the *Debarquement de Marie de Medis* in the Louvre. It is said that Cézanne even carried about with him wherever he went a copy. It was probably this influence that led Cézanne to make so many attempts to paint compositions of bathers."

Cézanne's models, from another viewpoint, too, were his despair. He painted slowly and only after mature deliberation over the probable effect of laying one color alongside another. Sometimes there was as much as a quarter of an hour between brush strokes. Sitters for portraits could not keep still, and that exasperated him. Flowers would wither, and sometimes he resorted to artificial flowers. Apples were satisfactory — they are slow to decay — and Cézanne painted bushels of them.

Vollard tells amusingly of his own experience as a sitter. One day when Cézanne was in good humor, he asked him to paint his portrait, and the master consented. A sitting was arranged for the following day.

"Upon arriving, I saw a chair in the middle of the studio, arranged on a packing case, which was in turn supported by four rickety legs. I surveyed the platform with misgiving. Cézanne divined my apprehension. 'I prepared the model stand with my own hands. Oh, you won't run the least risk of falling, Monsieur Vollard, if you just keep your balance. Anyway, you mustn't budge an inch when you pose!'

"Seated at last — and with such care — I watched myself carefully in order not to make a single false move; in fact I sat absolutely motionless; but my very immobility brought on in the end a drowsiness against which I struggled successfully a long time. At last, however, my head dropped over on my shoulder, the balance was destroyed, and the chair, the packing-case and I all crashed to the floor together! Cézanne pounced upon me. 'You wretch! You've spoiled the pose. Do I have to tell you again you must sit like an apple? Does an apple move?' From that day on, I adopted the plan of drinking a cup of black coffee before going for a sitting; as an added precaution, Cézanne would watch me attentively, and, if he thought he saw signs of fatigue or symptoms of sleep, he had a way of looking at me so significantly that I returned immediately to the pose like an angel — I mean like an apple. An apple never moves!"

Cézanne cared little about his model. More than any painter before him, he concentrated on paint. He had no story to tell, no sermon to preach.

Yet, he was not ready to tear himself away from the natural appearance of things, like the Cubists and the other artists of the abstract that followed him. He aimed to express the eternal solidity of things — a landscape, a human form, an apple — anything would do. The model was unimportant; what he brought out of himself and gave to the model was the big thing. He was the first of the Expressionists. The day of the Impressionists, with their catching of the exquisite, fleeting, external appearance of the moment was at an end. A mightier painter than Raphael had arisen — Raphael had told the divine story of the Madonna by sketching the lovely head of his girl mistress. Cézanne eclipsed Raphael's Madonna with — an apple.

"MODERN ART" AND "WAR TIME MADNESS"

I T was with the advent of the *Fauves* — the "wild beasts" of the lairs of Montmartre — that "Modernism" of the brand agitating America today began to make a noise in Paris. The prowlings of the *Fauves* started with about the dawn of the present century. The mystic word "Cézanne" began to be blazoned everywhere.

"Impressionism", after a struggle of forty years, was settling down to enjoy a quiet, undisturbed, well-earned possession of the academies it had wrested from the hands of painters of smooth, structureless nudes — painters like Bouguereau and Cabanel. The old opposition was not entirely dead, but its struggles were of the feebleness of the last gasps.

And then the clatter and din arose.

We didn't hear a great deal of it in America until the famous Armory show in New York and Chicago in the spring of 1913.

In accordance with well-defined habits of confusion in the minds of old maids (female and male), who, unfortunately, are our most numerous art mentors, the din of the Armory show is intermingled now with the din of the World War that broke out a year later. The "anarchism" and the "bolshevism" of the new art is confused in their minds, consequently, with the "red" political activities that caused such a mighty bustling about of their cousin in high place, A. Mitchell Palmer.

In the fifteen years that have elapsed, these old maids (female and male) are proclaiming the "art madness" an outgrowth of the "war madness". In my possession is an indignant letter written by one of the veteran female art critics of Chicago, informing me, after a long tirade against Toulouse-Lautrec, Van Gogh, and Gauguin, whose paintings in the Art Institute of Chicago I had ventured to admire in print, that "their unbalance was part of the madness of war times."

Coming from so authoritative a source, this was exciting news — positively psychic — seeing that Van Gogh put a bullet through his poor tortured breast in 1890, that Gauguin succumbed to too much tropics and Tahitian love in 1903, and that Toulouse-Lautrec passed from the scenes of his night prowlings in Paris in 1901. The World War, according to some of our best historians, broke out in the summer of 1914.

Gauguin, Van Gogh and Toulouse-Lautrec were as "mad" as any of the "Moderns", and so was Cézanne, the greatest of them all, who died in 1906, eight years before the Kaiser started his famous month's march from Berlin to Paris, via Belgium.

But let us examine the activities of the later "wild men"— Henri Matisse, for example, to whom was originally applied the term *Fauve* that came to comprehend his gang; Pablo Picasso, inventor of "Cubism", wildest of the "war madnesses"; Marie Laurencin, who has an unfortunate habit of forgetting to paint noses in the faces of her pretty girls, to the distress of the old maids (female and male); Emil Nolde, wild man of the caverns of Munich; Paul Klee, babbling "Dadaist", who might pose, according to the old maids (female and male), for the hero in the final tableau of Ibsen's "Ghosts".

For sensational "madness", Matisse never went beyond the tortured, writhing-hipped *"Odalisque"*, which was in the Quinn collection and was the prize of the Paris auction sale of that collector's effects after his death; never beyond "The Dance" of 1910; never beyond the "Studio Interior", recently added to Dr. Barnes' collection at Merion, Pa.; never beyond "Music", a companion piece to the "Dance". All these were completed between 1907 and 1911, and were famous before the fatal midsummer of 1914.

By 1913, the Cubists were so well defined as a group that Guillaume Apollinaire published in Paris his *"Meditations Esthetiques — Les Peintres Cubistes"*. The painters discussed, who had done significant work as Cubists at least a year before the outbreak of the World War with its "war-time madness", were: Pablo Picasso, Georges Braque, Jean Metzinger, Albert Gleizes, Juan Gris, Marie Laurencin, Fernand Leger, Francis Picabia, Marcel Duchamp, Duchamp Villon.

Picasso's Cubism was well defined as early as 1909, and he never did anything "wilder" in the method than his "Man with the Clarinet", 1912.

Nolde, the Munich "wild man", who hasn't yet invaded us, and who will make our critical eyes pop out when he does, is no wilder today than he was in 1899. Some of the most terrific of his illustrations of Biblical and religious episodes were done before the outbreak of the war —"Christ in the Underworld", for example, in 1911, and "Holy Night" in 1912.

But the most astonishing fact to be recorded is that "Dadaism" itself isn't the product of "war-time madness". This discovery is a little disappointing — there would be something psychologically fit about the babble of "Dadaism" being a reaction from the tension of war — something Ibsenish.

But the painful documents are at hand. Paul Klee was doing "Dada" things as early, at least, as 1910. The "Dadaists" haven't improved yet on his "Seven Maidens" of that year. The newspapers were making a sensation of "Dada" about the period of the Armistice. The reporters were a decade behind the "wild men" of the studios.

PAUL CEZANNE

The newspaper furore over the Armory show of 1913 became mingled with the furore of the World War, and it is not to be wondered at that there should be confusion of the two in the popular mind. That there is confusion in the minds of the "critics" is open to various explanations. The most charitable of these is crass ignorance — and there is no ignorance more desperately crass than that of art "critics". A less charitable view is that writers and lecturers hating and fearing "Modern Art" have yielded to a temptation sometimes too strong for even "statesmen" to resist — to take advantage of a popular mistake and magnify it in the interest of the destruction of a detested cause.

For the last ten years of his life, Cézanne was a mild sensation in Paris, taken seriously by a few, ridiculed by more, and ignored by the great generality. It was not until Matisse and his *Fauves* began to make their noise that Cézanne was really discovered.

Matisse, then 31, exhibited for the first time with the Independents in their Salon of 1901, and the clatter started soon afterward. By 1908, he was a veteran *Fauve*, and it was in April of that year that Alfred Stieglitz brought the first of his canvases to America, and exhibited them in his famous "291"— the immortal little "Photo-Secession Gallery", 291 Fifth Avenue, New York — the only focal point of "Modern Art" in America until the Armory show.

November, 1906, marks the opening of "291".

The first show was of modernistic photography, Stieglitz being a camera artist. In 1907, there was staged a show of drawings by Rodin, then regarded as so "wild" that he aroused the intense indignation of American painters like Chase and Alexander. The Matisse show the following year, of course, brought a recurrence of red wrath — the sort still meted out to Matisse as late as the retrospective show of his work in New York and Chicago in 1927. To keep indignation at a white heat for twenty years is, in itself, an achievement.

The "war-time madness" of even the critics is thus seen to have antedated, in America, the war by fully seven years.

The *"Fauves"* won a quicker and more decisive victory in Paris than did their predecessors, the Impressionists, whom they have supplanted not only in the art capital but throughout all Continental Europe. Matisse and Picasso and their fellows are not as yet completely victorious themselves, but their recently dead heroes for whom they fought are — Cézanne, Gauguin and Van Gogh. The *"Fauves"*, however, are so assured themselves of academic acceptance that the restless younger rebels are already at work on the counter-revolution. Art, to remain alive, cannot stand still.

OF *Abstraction, Distortion and Ridiculous* "EXPERTS"

THE point that seems to worry the enemies of "Modernism" most is the insistence by the artist on his right to abstract design — an insistence that led to the riotous bursting of all bounds in the early days of Post-Impressionism — that luxuriated in the wild distortions of the German Expressionists, and culminated in Cubism — the highest point of the "insanity" of the "crazy clowns" and "mountebanks", as they have been styled by their foes.

The abstract is no newer, however, than the other salient features of "Modernism". It is discovered in drawings of the pre-historic reindeer hunters in the caves of the Pyrenees. It is the very essence of Byzantine art — perhaps the most brilliant expression of pure art the world has ever known — and it is a basic principle of the art of the Chinese, about which our "critics"

[59]

and museum lecturers are wont to rave — without having the remotest inkling of what the Chinese were driving at.

A curiously ridiculous manifestation of the ignorance of American "art experts" as to the uses and beauty of the abstract occurred during the winter of 1926-27 in the dispute between the United States, as represented by its customs officials in New York, and the French sculptor, Constantin Brancusi, one of the best of contemporary masters of abstract beauty.

Brancusi sent from Paris to America a number of pieces of his sculpture — marbles, bronzes and carved wood — for exhibition and possible sale in this country. When they arrived at the New York customs, the officials were puzzled over the queer objects that presented themselves to their untutored gaze. "Experts" were called in, Brancusi's sculptures failed of classification as "art", and a duty was imposed upon the metal objects as "utilitarian".

"In charging Constantin Brancusi $4,000 duty on the bronzes which he brought to America to exhibit and sell", reported Forbes Watson, art critic of the New York World, and editor of the monthly magazine The Arts, "the New York office maintained that the position taken by it in this matter was based upon the advice of the 'highest authorities' in art. Marcel Duchamp, who acted as Mr. Brancusi's agent during the exhibition in New York and Chicago, invited the editor of The Arts to accompany him to the customs house to enter a protest at the time when the idea of charging Mr. Brancusi a duty first came up. Accompanied by Henry McBride and Marcel Duchamp I went to keep the appointment made with the proper customs house official. One of the questions we were asked was whether Daniel Chester French would consider that the 'Bird in Flight' and similar bronzes by Brancusi are sculpture. One of the answers given was: 'Certainly not, nor would Mr. Brancusi consider any of the works of Mr. Daniel Chester French sculpture.' And yet it was apparent that the customs official thought that Daniel Chester French was one of the 'highest authorities'."

Mr. Watson devoted most of his time "during the discussion with the customs house official, who, incidentally, stated quite frankly that he knew nothing about art, trying to point out to him that whereas Mr. Daniel Chester French and his associates who are so much favored by the fine arts commission in Washington, under the chairmanship of Mr. A. C. Moore, might condemn Brancusi's work quite honestly, if not impartially, as not being sculpture, their condemnation means nothing, because they are incapable of understanding the artistic intention of Mr. Brancusi. It was pointed out by Marcel Duchamp and Henry McBride that Brancusi obviously did not have in mind an object of utilitarian use when he created his 'Bird in Flight'.

He was attempting to create a beautiful sculptural form.

"The United States customs official was asked several times why it was necessary to go beyond this intention on the part of the artist and the vain effort was made to explain to him that a high degree of elimination does not constitute a reason for condemning a work of art. The customs house official could have proved, by an examination of Mr. Brancusi's work as a whole, that Mr. Brancusi, whatever his greatness or lack of greatness might be, was certainly motivated by esthetic rather than practical intentions, but I think the 'high authorities' had already done their work."

The dispute attracted international notice, and was a sad commentary on the state of art understanding in America.

In "Bird in Flight", typical of Brancusi at his best, the sculptor insists only, like his fellow Modernists, in recording his emotional reactions to his model, instead of making a photographic record. His Bird may be regarded as analogous to the Wild Rose of the music composer Edward MacDowell. In candy store windows devoted to Easter displays can be seen whole flocks of chocolate and marshmallow chickens, ducks, pigeons and doves that are more readily recognizable as representations of birds than Brancusi's polished bronze, and Mr. Brancusi, being a man of normal human intelligence — despite allegations of "critics" and "sculptors"— would probably acknowledge as much if pinned down to a confession by customs officials and their "expert advisers". But, you can also buy at the ten-cent store a crinoline rose for your coat lapel that will be of more service to you in identifying beside the roadside on a Sunday auto spin a wild rose, if you happen not to know what one looks like, than even a symphony orchestral rendition of MacDowell's "To a Wild Rose".

Brancusi in developing his "Bird in Flight", which is a lovely cylindrical form, tapering at both ends and swelling in the middle, with only a faint suggestion of wings and head, departed no further from rational representation of something existent in nature than did Hogarth in describing his famous "Line of Beauty."

Hogarth, in a moment of profitable idleness, drew one day a curve that so thrilled him that he wrote two large volumes descriptive of its grace and its emotional possibilities. This line is somewhat of the shape of the letter "S" lying nearly flat. Hogarth inscribed it on a palette, and used it as a signature, just as Whistler afterward employed his famous butterfly. Hogarth's "Line of Beauty" is just as abstract and devoid of rational pictorial qualities as Brancusi's "Bird in Flight", and has no better right to exist as an art entity than Brancusi's graceful sculpture — and no worse.

The fact that Brancusi derived his abstract form of loveliness from an actual bird is what worries customs house officials, "art experts", "critics", museum lecturers, prominent-members-of-art-clubs-consulted-by-newspaper-reporters-for-an-opinion-when-a-controversy-arises, and other of the thick-headed gentry who do not seem to be able to get through their skulls the fact that abstract loveliness can be a goal toward which to reach out — a goal perhaps more worthy than the making of a life-like wax figure for Madame Tussaud's collection.

The attainment of this goal through simplification and alteration of lines of the human body has been, at any rate, a very serious aim of great artists throughout the ages. Brancusi has done it in that exquisite torso and head, popularly styled "The Princess Bonaparte", which was taken out of a Paris display by the police because of a fancied phallic resemblance, but which was allowed to be exhibited in both New York and Chicago — probably because the police in these cities don't know what the word "phallic" means or haven't enough imagination to detect the resemblance. Our Chicago police women, sent not long ago to get evidence for the arrest of a Chicago book dealer for displaying for sale pornographic postcards, triumphantly purchased a colored reproduction of Giorgione's "Sleeping Venus".

Archipenko is another present-day sculptor who has evolved forms of great abstract beauty from the nude female torso, elongating the body somewhat after

CONSTANTIN BRANCUSI LE BAISER

the manner of El Greco, though with different intent and spirit.

Once the right to abstract design is admitted — an admission conservative critics and artists of America will fail to make, even on their death beds — the bars are thrown down to distortion, the terrible bugaboo of Conservatism.

Yet, distortion occurs freely in the art accepted as normal by its foes. The unbroken graceful curve of the line of the nose and the eyebrow of classic Greek sculpture, for example, is a "distortion" in that it does not occur in nature.

"Raphael's 'Saint Michael' in the Louvre has a thigh half a mile long", Renoir told his biographer Vollard. "But it might not be so fine otherwise. Take Michelangelo himself, the supreme anatomist. The other day, I was afraid that the breasts of my Venus were too far apart. Just then I happened upon a photograph of the 'Dawn' from the tomb of Julian de' Medici. Then I saw that Michelangelo had not hesitated to put the breasts even farther apart than I had."

The distortions of El Greco are resented by the Conservatives almost as sharply as those of Cézanne, because El Greco is a high god in the modern Pantheon; but he is no more a distortionist than Botticelli, who somehow or other manages to retain his respectability, even though he has been drawn upon freely by Picasso and more especially by Modigliani.

The "old masters" did not hesitate any more than the new to alter the natural lines and curves of the human body if by that means they could better the beauty or strengthen the emotional appeal of their designs.

Byzantine art offers, perhaps, the most thoroughly understandable employment of the abstract in the representation of the human face and form. This art is the one bright development of the Dark Ages, when Europe lay under the heavy pall of superstition, fear, and sullen obedience to ignorant priestly authority. It struggled against the heaviest odds to an attainment that lies beyond the goal of even the most capable of the "Moderns".

Christianity, Mohammedanism and Judaism, at sword points with each other, combined to enforce the command thundered from Sinai by Moses, to whose authority they all bent: "Thou shalt not make unto thee any graven image."

Mohammed had reiterated the command so emphatically that Islam artists dared only experiment with a certain series of initial letters, so deeply mysterious that God only, according to the priests, knew the meaning. The lavish ornamentation of these letters, with the fine mathematical imagination of the Arabs, resulted in the brilliant decoration of the Alhambra — in the amazingly beautiful designs of Persian carpets.

Christians, especially those of Jewish extraction and those who took the Mosaic books as seriously as they took their gospels, were scarcely more liberal in their interpretation of the decree of Moses than were the followers of the arch-fiend of Islam — but there was a difference. Had not the face of Christ, according to tradition, been imprinted on the handkerchief of St. Veronica? Also, in the early liberal days, under the Roman Peter — who, unfortunately for the world, lost supremacy to Paul, the William Jennings Bryan of antiquity — Christians in the catacombs had sketched their Master freely on the walls, and had done Him in mosaic.

These traditional manifestations of pictorial art could not be downed completely by the gloomy fanatics of the Dark Ages, and so there developed, though under great difficulty, an art of representation that had to be very careful not to become so "naturalistic" as to be offensive. God, Christ and the Virgin were superhuman, though in the mold of men and women, and in their representation the painters had to watch that none of the sins of the flesh intruded. As late as the days of Velasquez, the Spanish Inquisition enforced rigid rules in this respect.

This Christian element met, in Byzantium, the Mohammedan element of ornate abstraction, and Byzantine art resulted. It was kept drastically ascetic in its representation of human flesh, but brilliant colors and highly ornamental lines were permissible in the draperies and the background.

Cimabue and Giotto, first of the Naturalists, broke the conventions, and paved the way for the Italian Renaissance, with its huge sledge-hammer nudes of Michelangelo and its honeyed Madonnas of Raphael — both human.

To the Byzantines El Greco harked back, and many of the "extravagances" of the "Moderns"— their abstractions and distortions — can be traced directly to the masters who flourished brilliantly in Constantinople through the Dark Ages.

"Critics", however, and museum lecturers, and picture makers among the painters cannot or will not see the connection, any more than they will admit an analogy between "Modernism" and the art of the Chinese. Byzantine art and Chinese art are "respectable" — but the art of Picasso and Matisse and Archipenko is not. The truth may slowly percolate into their brains, however, just as the truth with regard to Whistler has done. Most anyone now can see a resemblance between Whistler and Japanese prints, and will admit Whistler had a right to that source of inspiration.

If Byzantine and Chinese art are "respectable", however, another source of abstraction and distortion in "Modern Art" is not — namely, African sculpture. The Negro primitives are barred from respectability — not through any race prejudice, but because they were "discovered" and exploited by the *Fauves* of Paris before the learned historians of the Academy had got around to taking cognizance.

Matisse, Picasso, Modigliani, Derain and others of the "wild men" became enthusiastic over the strange and powerful forms evolved by the Congo Negroes before the professors got a chance to classify and explain them. Were it not for the professorial commentators, Solomon's gorgeously barbaric, lustful "Song of Songs" would have been expurgated out of the Bible long ago.

The foes of Negro sculpture are treading on the same uneasy grounds that lie under the feet of the enemies of all "Modernism". For the highly respectable Sphinx may be proven yet a manifestation of the primitive art of the woolly-headed Africans. The Negro sculpture the Modernists revel in, however, is of the Congo and of a much later period. Whatever its origin — Negro or Egyptian — the Sphinx is everything the foes of "Modernism" detest — abstract, distorted, Cubistic — magnificent!

"CUBISM"
the Great Anatomy Lesson

"CUBISM" is the great anatomy lesson of "Modernism".

Art stood in sore necessity of a drastic operation. From the days when the Carracci reduced Raphael to formula, the efforts of the academies were directed toward surface perfection.

"To hold, as 'twere, the mirror up to Nature", was the aim and end of art.

Bouguereau, with his marvelously smooth nudes — toward which the Italian "Moderns", by the way, are dangerously veering — the Bouguereau who kept Cézanne out of the Salon — may be looked upon as typical of the camera-like perfection to which art had attained just before the Impressionistic revolution. The rules had been perfected — there was no reason why the mechanics of art should not go along producing imitations of nature till the end of time.

But while this surface perfection was pleasant to look upon, art was rotting inside — an over-ripe, rosy apple, growing hectically red — a lovely, pallid woman, poetically pale, with a cancer gnawing at her vitals. Monet and his Impressionists did nothing to alleviate the condition — they rather aggravated it.

The knife of a surgeon was imperative — Cézanne made the incision.

"We must remake Poussin from Nature", was his challenge to the academies with their relentless rules.

"We must again become classicists by way of Nature, that is to say, by sensation", he explained again.

But the knife thrust that hit the vitals — the scalpel Picasso afterward turned in the wound — was the famous dictum: "Nature can be expressed by the cube, the cone, and the cylinder. Anyone who can paint these simple forms can paint Nature."

It was no new doctrine — Durer had not only expressed it, but had amplified it elaborately and completely, with regard to the human body. Rembrandt had used it in painting, and it was a commonplace in sculpture.

It was not, however, until Pablo Picasso and Georges Braque, in the autumn of 1908, exhibited in Paris some curiously geometrical pictures — Picasso's were human figures, Braque's landscapes — that the art world, morbidly sensitive from the brisk drubbings at the hands of Cézanne and the young upstarts known

[71]

as *Fauves,* became aware that a new irritant was being rubbed like salt into its wounds.

Cubisme, the amused Henri Matisse, already a celebrity, leader of the *Fauves,* pronounced the new pictures, which appealed to him then as insolent curiosities. *Cubisme,* the newspapers echoed, and a new sensation spread like wildfire, whose flames have not yet been quenched.

Cubism, like the other fundamentals, is as old as art itself. The Sphinx, as we have just affirmed, is Cubistic, as is all Egyptian art of the period of the pyramid builders. In drawing human figures, the Egyptians made no attempt at photographic realism. The face, in typical pictures, is in profile, with the eyes looking full-face at the beholder. The shoulders, in exact contradiction to the set of the head, are square to the front, and the legs and the feet are again in profile. This curious jumble of parts, put together to suggest a man, not to picture him, has been explained on the theory that the aspects of the various fragments of the body as presented are the aspects most impressive and most vividly remembered.

It is not from the Egyptian conventions, however, nor from the experiments of Durer that Cubism, in its modern manifestation, sprang, but from the musically-mathematical brain of Pablo Picasso, a Spanish painter resident in Paris, born and brought up amid the art relics of the Moorish occupation of his native Anda-

ARISTIDE MAILLOL   TORSO

lusia. Picasso, the most sensitive intellect since Leonardo da Vinci and the most adroit hand since Raphael, pondered Cézanne's cube-cone-cylinder dictum. With patterns of Mohammedan art firmly rooted in his childhood memory, with a mathematical instinct dominating his subconscious, and with music and musical instruments the passion of his leisure hours, he gave a new art form to the world.

Whatever extravagances it developed later, Cubism was, in its inception, the emotional expression of a first-rate genius who happened to be of a mathematical mind, and whose impressionable years happened to be spent in the shadows of the Alhambra, deathless monument to the art of the most highly cultured race of geometricians that ever walked the earth.

When Picasso began to paint his emotional reactions to his models — not the models themselves — his mathematical subconscious asserted itself, with its ornate yet severe Andalusian memories, and "Cubism" resulted. Had Picasso been brought up in Pasadena, California, with its annual tournament of roses as the most spectacular event in a child's life, his particular "wild art" might have resulted in "Roseism." Or, had he been reared in London, he might have produced "Fogism" — which couldn't have been any foggier to London than his Cubism has been.

The influence, too, of the accident of Picasso being a musician, has been far-reaching. In his very earliest boyhood he was fascinated day after day watching an old workman stringing violins and guitars and mandolins. He not only knows musical instruments as producers of sweet sounds, but he knows them intimately as structural entities. In seeking the soul — the essence of people and things — musical instruments and their parts are constantly intruding. Many of his compositions are frankly musical and so named, as his girls with mandolins and his men with clarinets. But even when he is doing things entirely without the range of music — as, for example, his portrait of Buffalo Bill and his study of a bottle of rum — musical motifs are plainly in evidence.

Picasso, the inventor, also set the pattern for Cubism, which has been followed too definitely by his disciples, prone to use the geometrical designs and the musical motifs without the good reason, or rather the spontaneous impulse of Picasso. Because of that fact, largely, the work of the majority of them is of no consequence — lacking in sincerity. The few men of genius who have experimented in the method have varied the technique of Picasso to fit their own individual reactions. Fernand Leger, perhaps the greatest of them, had a mechanical instead of an abstract mathematical soul, and his Cubistic pictures are fantastically alive with machinery. They have more dynamism than Picasso's — the Spaniard's pictures are for the most part stolid and still. Leger's are restless, ready to go.

[74]

The great difficulty in sensing Cubism is the almost universal attempt of the beholder to read into the pictures a "pictorial" quality. Cubism is the negation of the "pictorial"— the farthest excursion, in its extreme manifestations, art has ever gone in the direction of the abstract.

The artists themselves are not without blame for the confusion. They have "explained" how they have viewed their models from many different angles, and how they have even introduced time elements — a development today in the model that was not apparent yesterday—how they have extracted bits from all these impressions, thrown them helter-skelter into the "picture", and called it a day.

This "explanation" has been an invitation to the observer to try to "figure it out", much as he "figures out" how to put together the elements of a picture puzzle in the Sunday supplements.

Cubism is no such naturalistic puzzle — Cubism, that is, of Picasso and Leger and the men who count. All there is to the "picture" is what strikes the eye — as the designs on the walls of the Alhambra or in a Persian carpet. If you don't get an emotional reaction beholding the "picture" as it is, without trying to place the man's ear where it belongs in nature, or without trying to extract the G-string from the bottle of rum, then, for you, the picture is a failure.

As a matter of fact, Cubism has been found by

the artists themselves a popular failure, and its extreme manifestations have been all but abandoned.

That does not mean, as is often asserted, that the method itself has been thrown into the discard — it doesn't even mean that pure, undiluted Cubism has necessarily passed out of the art world forever. Fifty years from now — or a hundred — there may arise a genius, not mightier than Picasso, but of more tenacity — Picasso is a veritable art "tramp" of extraordinary versatility, roving from the most severely academic draftsmanship possessed by any living artist to the most astonishing vagaries — who will develop Cubism into a technique of universal acceptance like the technique of the Impressionists considered just as bizarre half a century ago.

Cubism at present is an element, greatly diluted and toned down, in practically all the art of the progressive "Moderns". The anatomy lesson has been learned, and learned well. Painters now know the guts of things as thoroughly as Bouguereau knew the skin.

Painting is returning definitely to the "pictorial" after the extreme vagaries of Cubism, Futurism, Vorticism, and the other "isms". But the artists of genius are "expressing" themselves emotionally in "pictures" as they did previously in "abstractions"— that is to say, they paint with a sense of the internal as well as the external.

One of the new Cubists, Andre Lhote, goes so

far as to combine, skillfully, Cubism with the severe Graeco-Roman Classicism of David.

The employment of Cubism as a rich and vital element in the new "pictorial" paintings is as though a clever, keen musician of "Tin Pan Alley" should take a wild strain of unearthly loveliness from Stravinsky and develop it into a tune. Maybe Gershwin has done it.

Now that the hullabaloo has died down — the tumult and the shouting receded into the far distance — Picasso's nightmareish fantasy appears as the substance of ethereal dreams. The theory of Picasso in spite of its outward trimmings of lunacy, in spite of its distortions by his disciples, was sound at the core — a method of frigid composition, delicate and decorative as blue-cold rock crystal, and mystic as death.

PABLO PICASSO:
A Footnote to Cubism

THE chances are that on that final midnight when
the blast of Gabriel's trumpet shall proclaim the end
of time and start his orchestra harping the Pollyanna
"Hosannah" of Eternity, the name of Pablo Picasso
will be found engraved on the blocks of Cubism.

Cubism, to change the figure, is the bed Picasso
designed for himself, and in it he must lie — to it he
must inevitably return, wherever he may roam, like
those princes of Fairyland doomed to spend appointed
hours of the day or the week or the year in the scene
of their crimes.

Cubism, however, is only one of the many manifestations of this amazing genius, whose versatility, indeed, is so astounding as to make him suspect even
among friends and fellows. His range is from the wildest vagaries of abstraction to the most correct of Natu-

ralism — and he has the faculty of changing his style overnight.

"Mountebank", he is called, with muttered oaths, by the puzzled watchers of his acrobatic leaps, his whirling gyrations — and mountebank he would be, were it not for the fact that whatever he does, he does with a sledge-hammer force, with an intensity of power, with a compressed emotionalism unique in contemporary art. In every one of his manifestations he has had his followers — eager disciples — artists of no mean abilities. Yet, compare their work with his, and note, in every instance, the difference between a commanding genius and an enthralled disciple. Whatever Picasso does, he does with terrific authority. His versatility, unmatched in the history of art through all the ages, is a phenomenon for enthusiasm, not for suspicion.

As early as 1905, Picasso, who was born in Malaga in 1881, was doing deathless pictures. To this year belong those vivid circus things, such as *"La Famille de l'Arlequin"*, *"Acrobates"*, *"Les Saltimbanques"*— expressions of the life of that particular phase of Bohemia unique in the annals of art. The Spaniard of 24 was already a master, assured and not to be questioned.

His development was much earlier, however, than even this. At 19, in the first year of the new century, he did a head of a woman that is still a favorite with enthusiasts for the mature Picasso. To 1903 belongs his amazing *"La Soupe"*, a mother holding out a bowl of soup to her little daughter, that Daumier himself need not have been ashamed to claim, and that is redolent of the "primitive" impulse that has so directed Picasso's development.

Picasso has had his "periods", more or less distinctly defined, "Blue", "Rose", "Negroid", "Cubistic", "Naturalistic". He has been cursed for his pitifully attenuated figures of drinkers in the cafes of Paris — men and women, cheeks hollow, bones protruding. He has been as roundly cursed for his heavy female nudes — mountainous creatures that outweigh Renoir and Rubens. When he has hit the happy medium as to proportions he has still been cursed — for always is he Picasso, enemy of the Academy. Always is there a spirit that refuses to conform to formula, a spirit that excites the antagonism of souls that cannot get in step with the heart beat of Negro sculpture, of Byzantine Virgins, of portraits on Egyptian coffin lids.

Picasso, generally, is placid and passive on the surface — the true stoicism of the Primitive, in whom the fires of hell are smouldering. It is this suppressed fire that is his strength, that arouses antagonisms in breasts that cannot understand — that can feel only a dull hate, in sensing something vaguely fearsome.

This dynamite-loaded placidity Picasso carries even into Cubism, which is the better comprehended when viewed in connection with the other works of the varied "periods". His Cubism has been styled poetical — lyric.

PABLO PICASSO   LA FAMILLE DE L'ARLEQUIN

Poetical it is, and lyric — if your ideas of lyricism comprehend Shelley and Heine.

Almost from his advent in the world of art — assuredly since his invention of Cubism — Picasso has been in the limelight. He has been a target for ridicule, like the other "wild men", but somehow his strength has been sensed even by the satirists, and there has been a certain fear mingled with the sport — bear-baiting, rather than punching the haunches of a "trick mule".

Picasso, however, like Matisse, has a tough hide. He has proceeded calmly on his way, letting the curs bark at his heels to their hearts' content. Today, like Matisse, he is a "best seller". Tomorrow — he will be with Cézanne, and Manet, and Chardin, and El Greco, and Rembrandt — and the Ages.

MATISSE:
A *"Fauve"* in Process
of Canonization

HENRI MATISSE, like Pablo Picasso, refuses to rest under his laurels. Twelve years the senior of the Spaniard, and in a period of life when years sit less lightly — he was born in 1869 — this Frenchman, as late as 1926, when a goodly number of his pictures came under our observation, was producing work that ranks with his best.

Matisse and Picasso are the two painters since Cézanne of assured position high in the Pantheon of the Modern Renaissance — the greatest movement in art history since the Italian awakening. Gauguin, Van Gogh and Renoir were contemporaries of the arch revolutionist of Aix.

As this survey of the Modern movement was being made, there was current in the galleries of the Arts Club of Chicago — the livest art organization, without exception, in America — a retrospective show of Matisse, 1890-1926, assembled and staged a few weeks before in New York by the F. Valentine Dudensing Gallery, with Pierre Matisse, son of the painter, one of the moving spirits.

The show at the Arts Club, through one of the decrees of the satiric gods with dramatic instinct, occurred simultaneously with the 1927 official annual exhibition at the Art Institute of paintings by artists of Chicago and vicinity. The local show was particularly dull and old-fashioned — even for this annual affair — having been juried this time by three out-of-town museum directors, cautious and ultra-conservative as small-city directors are apt to be, with their rich patrons always on their necks. The drama was heightened by the further fact that there was at the Art Institute, in a gallery set aside there for this same Arts Club of Chicago, a display of Chardin's paintings assembled by the Wildenstein galleries — Chardin whose onions and joints of beef match Cézanne's apples. Chardin was the painter of the kitchen — Cézanne of the dining room.

Back in 1890, it was revealed in comparison of these three fateful simultaneous exhibitions, Matisse could have qualified for the Chicago artists' show of 1927. The difference was, Matisse had progressed in thirty-six years, while official art in Chicago had only caught up with the world procession of 1890, three years before the immortal World's Fair, that made us an "international art center", and made the clique who got in control as the result of the fame of the art display at the fair solid for a third of a century. Only now are the fingers of this clique being definitely pried loose from the strangle hold they have held — only now is Chicago waking thoroughly to the fact that the glamors of 1893 are as dead as the glories of Greece and the grandeur of Rome.

In the Matisse retrospective exhibition, there was a little still life dated 1890, the earliest complete work the painter has saved, that could probably have got past even the small-city museum directors who selected the simultaneous Chicago show. It was executed in the days before Matisse began to froth at the mouth — the days before he became leader of the *Fauves*.

The utterly asinine contention of enemies of Modernism that the new masters are "unable to draw", that they produce their "wild" art after the fashion of little children because they can do no better, crumbles to dust in the presence of so thoroughly correct an academic piece of work as this still life.

All Modernists — it cannot be insisted too often — worthy of the name are past masters in the fundamentals. Picasso, with all the alleged vagaries of Cubism, is the most expert draftsman since Raphael, and Matisse is not far behind him.

The little still life of 1890, which Matisse prizes

highly, with probably the amused fondness of a man of middle life looking back on a youthful love affair, was very much superior to anything in the rival show of the Chicago artists — in much the same method of that show. Its inclusion in the retrospective exhibition made rather difficult for once the favorite phrase of our Chicago "critics", museum lecturers and prominent members of art clubs consulted by newspaper reporters, that Matisse "can't draw".

Back in 1890, when he painted this still life, Matisse, a man of 21, had little thought of a professional career as an artist. He was a law student, taking drawing lessons on the side, merely for the fun of it.

Two years later, he went from his home in Northern France to Paris to complete his law studies, but found painting so much more fascinating that he abandoned his prospective career, and entered the school of Beaux Arts. His masters there — queer as it may sound in the light of later developments — were Gustave Moreau, great as a teacher, however low his once popular paintings have fallen in critical estimation; Bouguereau, arch-enemy of Cézanne, consistently keeping the Hermit of Aix out of the Salon; Gerome, melodramatic painter of harems, and Ferrier.

Under their instruction, Matisse became so thoroughly an Academician that the French government commissioned him to copy old masters in the Louvre on orders from other museums that desired exact duplicates. The still life in the Arts Club show demonstrates a budding fitness for these commissions.

"I studied in the schools mornings, and copied at the Louvre in the afternoons for ten years", Matisse once told a newspaper interviewer. "I made copies for the government, but when I introduced some of my own emotional impressions, or personal translations of the pictures, the government did not care to buy; it only wanted a photographic copy."

It was this impulse toward emotionalism that cut Matisse adrift from his moorings in the harbor of Academism and the still life of 1890, and led him through a series of glorious adventures, whose end is not yet, as was demonstrated in two dazzling *"Odalisques"* in the retrospective show, dated 1926.

"If one feels no emotion, one should not paint", he told his newspaper interviewer, quoted in Arthur Jerome Eddy's "Cubists and Post-Impressionism."

"I know how to draw correctly, having studied form so long. I now draw with feeling and not anatomically. While working, I never try to think, only to feel. I only make studies from models, not to use in a picture, but to strengthen my knowledge; and I never draw from a previous sketch or study, but from memory.

"I have a class of sixty pupils"— (this interview is dated 1913; Matisse quit teaching a little later) — "and make them draw accurately, as a student always should do at the beginning. I do not encourage them to work as I do now.

"I began at the *Ecole des Beaux Arts*. When I opened my studio years after, for some time I painted just like anyone else. But things didn't go at all, and I was very unhappy. Then, little by little, I began to paint as I felt. One cannot do successful work which has much feeling unless one sees the subject very simply, and one must do this in order to express one's self as clearly as possible."

Whistler, seeing for the first time Cézanne's portrait of Mlle. Cézanne, his sister, remarked: "If a 6-year-old child had drawn that on his slate, his mother, if she were a good mother, would have whipped him."

Matisse went Whistler's conception of Cézanne one better. He was accused of drawing like a child of 5. "That is what I am trying to do", he replied; "I should like to recapture that freshness of vision which is characteristic of extreme youth, when all the world is new to it."

When, however, fond mammas wander into the Arts Club's galleries or stumble into the famous Birch-Bartlett room of modern paintings at the Art Institute of Chicago, and declare their offspring, just learning to use a lead pencil, draws things exactly like those of Matisse or Modigliani, they are suffused with a density of fog such as hangs round one of our Chicago art critics who announced he thoroughly understood Brancusi, and then went off into the usual doddering discourse of haters of Modernism who attempt to explain its manifestations without so much as an inkling of the Expressionistic aims.

The naivete of Matisse is a naivete only of vision — his execution is guided by a skill that the thoroughly saturated academician cannot even comprehend — a skill of sophistication that has learned its trade under the iron heel of discipline, and then cast off all shackles. Even more "childishly foolish" things are done by the German Expressionists — Georg Grosz, for example. When Grosz gets through, his 3-year-old infant drawings are the most hellish satires of all time — unsurpassed even by the innocent childish babbling of Gulliver.

The late James Huneker, no very warm friend of the "Modernists"— (for him, as for our "critics" and museum lecturers, everything since Monet is practically a blank —"crazy clowns", he called the Cubists, and the Futurists and Neo-Impressionists were "charlatans and mediocrities") — nevertheless had an intuitive perception of the genius of Matisse.

"Matisse", he observes in "Steeplejack", "has confessed: 'I condense the signification of the body by looking for the essential lines', which is slightly different from the cockney Cubists and their chatter about 'significant form'. Mr. Berenson has pronounced Matisse to be 'a magnificent draftsman and a great designer'. The

HENRI MATISSE   ODALISQUE

Chinese are his masters, also the masters of the world in art, though we are only beginning to find it out. Japan, which originates nothing, borrows its art from the older kingdom. I don't care whether Matisse is a Poster-Impressionist, a sensitivist, expressivist, or a snark, but I do know that he is a master of line that, as Frank Mather, Jr., asserts, has had no superior since the time of Pollajuolo and the Florentines. What if the concubinage of his colors screams in rhythms that make the flesh creep? There is power, profound sophistication, subtle rhythm, all couched in novel terms. He can be suavely harmonious. He is sometimes as sunny as Mozart or Monet."

Except that Matisse derives rather from the Persian than the Chinese, and except that he has a very real sensitiveness for the "significant form" of the "crazy clowns", Huneker has done a rather good job defending himself from the accusations of "optical degeneration" he was said to be suffering when he dared in those pioneer days to say a good word for Matisse.

Speaking of "crazy clowns", it was Matisse, as we have already stated, who first held the Cubists up to good-natured ridicule by giving them the name that has stuck. The leader of the *Fauves* back in 1908 didn't quite comprehend what the youngsters Picasso and Braque were driving at with their queer geometry. That he has since learned is quite evident in the retrospective show, as, for example, in the nude *Odalisque* of 1926.

He is not a builder in color, like Cézanne. He is more the decorator, like Gauguin. However, he has Cézanne's extraordinarily sensitive feeling for subtle and delicate blendings of shades and tones, instead of Gauguin's superb anarchy of reds and greens and blues flung violently down beside each other.

That Matisse has lost nothing of his cunning in either line or color is evident in his two *Odalisques* of 1926. They display a splendor of richness, adroit invention and verve unsurpassed by anything in the long gamut of his show, covering a third of a century.

Some idea of the "childish carelessness" of Matisse's drawing may be gathered from the history of his *Grand Nu* — the most stunning female figure he has ever painted, and which he has also lithographed. This canvas was not displayed in the retrospective show, but the lithograph has been exhibited at the Albert Roullier galleries in Chicago and at Weyhe's, New York. Its execution occupied a period of about three years, during which Matisse made something over eight hundred drawings of his model.

Matisse, while still a *Fauve* to the great majority of American painters, is becoming nevertheless something of a "grand old man" of France, since the death of the former arch-rebel, Claude Monet. Matisse, now well along toward 60, may live to see himself a painfully respected idol.

Already there are signs.

[92]

For instance: During the summer of 1927 (and for succeeding summers since) his studio was placed on the itinerary of personally conducted parties of school teachers taken abroad by museum lecturers to see the art and culture of Europe in sixty or ninety days.

For instance again: During a recent visit to Chicago of Pierre Matisse, Henri's son, there was introduced to him one of our leading female conservative painters, who happens to be also a museum lecturer on occasions. She gushed and gurgled to Pierre her intense admiration for his father's work — which, in her museum tours she had been in the habit of ignoring or pointing out with detestation. Pierre was something of a social lion, and the painter-lecturer, in order to be in on the lionizing, had to go on record as admiring Henri — and, of course, she must continue to admire Henri to the end of her days.

These are a couple of straws in the wind that point to the sadly respectable canonization of a painter once so brilliant as a rebel.

OF GAUGUIN, *the Babbitt,* AND VAN GOGH, *the Evangelist*

THE *fin de siècle* was accompanied by much sage shaking of the head and lugubrious gutturals from those who had at heart the fate of all the arts — literature and sculpture, music and painting. Decadence and disaster were all they could sense. Monet and Rodin were as exotic — dilettanti — as Baudelaire and Ibsen. It was the autumn of art — a yellow and hectic red soon to shrivel and fade, and then would come a long, long winter of utter barrenness.

The critical pall-bearers were carrying art to the grave, chanting dolorously, when the sharp, quick, crisp yelps of Matisse and his fellow wild beasts of the lairs of Paris interrupted. The pall-bearers stopped indignantly to listen, and then to beat back the gleaming-eyed intruders, and while they were so engaged, the corpse got up and escaped.

The world's debt to Matisse does not end with its appreciation of his own paintings. It was the agitation of the *Fauves,* as we have indicated, that brought Cézanne into his inheritance — which he did not live to appreciate and to enjoy, dying in 1906 when he was only in the process of being established as the prophet of the new order —"the primitive of the way".

The searchlight of the *"Fauves"* revealed at the same time two other giant figures, Paul Gauguin, "poor wretch", dying in the Marquesas Islands in 1903, "his legs one great sore; his heart an ulcer", as Robert Rey expresses it; and Vincent Van Gogh, who put a bullet into his breast in 1890 to still the throbbing of his addled head.

Gauguin and Van Gogh, though widely different in their art aims and accomplishments, and though almost diametrically opposed as men — Gauguin, the pagan, seeking personal as well as artistic freedom among savage women of the Pacific islands; Van Gogh, deserting the pulpit because he thought he could give more fervid expression to his evangelistic message in paint — these two fanatical geniuses were drawn together by irresistible impulse and became so closely associated for a time that their names are linked as firmly as Damon and Pythias — David and Jonathan.

Prominently identified with "Post-Impressionism" at its inception — though Van Gogh was long dead and Gauguin was dying when the movement began to make a noise in the world — the private lives and morals of these two gave the enemies of the cause a weapon they did not hesitate to use — to use unfairly — and to keep on using, even unto this day. Thus, when Kenyon Cox declares the revolutionists "committed suicide or died in madhouses", he has Van Gogh to point to as evidence. The plural doesn't greatly worry Mr. Cox and his friends.

When the new artists were characterized as frightfully immoral, a menace to civilization, Gauguin could always be rung in to justify the charge.

Cézanne was a quiet, peaceful, shy sort of a country gentleman. All that the enemies of the new art could think up to fix upon him definitely was that he was an "anarchist"— this unobtrusive son of a wealthy banker, who never had any great worries about money, seeing that his father supplied him, and who probably could scarcely at any time have named the personnel of the ministry of France. They said, too, he was a "moron"— this constant haunter of the Louvre, who, as a boy, had consistently taken prizes in school above his brilliant fellow-student, Zola. Cézanne, too afraid of women to employ nude models, and seldom seen in female company, is nevertheless rated sexually immoral, in the vague estimate of our present-day spinster "critics" of art — spinsters male and female, married and unmarried — we have all varieties. For, is he not

PAUL GAUGUIN

closely associated in the art movement with Gauguin, who deserted his wife for the dark ladies of the Pacific, and with Van Gogh, who cut off his ear and presented it to an Arlesian prostitute?

Van Gogh, having been made a plural by Kenyon Cox — committing suicide on various occasions and dying in various madhouses — is also endowed by Joseph Pennell, another valiant battler against Modernism, with a wholesale mania for cutting off ears.

"And while I was in Arles", relates Pennell in "The Adventures of an Illustrator", "Van Gogh was there — *le fou* — who every month or so had a mission to cut off somebody's ears, and when the devil entered into him he would be locked up in his room with his paints. There he could make masterpieces that were not wanted, till one day in Auvers nobody was round to have their ears cut off, so he cut his own throat or shot himself."

It is, of course, Pennell's idea of "wit" — crude even for this boorish disciple of Whistler, who imagined himself in a class with the master of cutting satire. But the whole implication is meant to be nasty to the memory of Van Gogh, whose "masterpieces that were not wanted" — well, two of the very ones made at Arles, "The Yellow Room" and *La Berceuse,* are in the Birch-Bartlett collection in the Art Institute of Chicago, and Mr. Bartlett is envied by the knowing because

[97]

his large fortune enabled him to pick up two such expensive "documents in madness."

The incident of the severed ear is one of the vividly tragic stories in the annals of art. Gauguin tells about it in his "Intimate Journals"— a book outranking even "Noa Noa" for literary vividness, but available for English readers only in an edition "privately printed for subscribers only".

It was the culmination of the association of Gauguin and Van Gogh at Arles — an association to the advantage of both in the development of their art — an advantage Gauguin acknowledges, though he intimates he gave Van Gogh more than he received in turn — an intimation probably not justified by the facts. It was while they were living together at Arles that Van Gogh's madness began noticeably to develop.

"During the latter days of my stay," Gauguin relates, "Vincent would become excessively rough and noisy, and then silent. On several nights I surprised him in the act of getting up and coming over to my bed. To what can I attribute my awakening just at that moment?

"At all events it was enough for me to say to him, quite sternly, 'What's the matter with you, Vincent?' for him to go back to bed without a word and fall into a heavy sleep.

"The idea occurred to me to do his portrait while he was painting the still-life he loved so much — some ploughs. When the portrait was finished, he said to me: 'It certainly is I, but it's I gone mad.'

"That very evening he went to the cafe. He took a light absinthe. Suddenly he flung the glass and its contents at my head. I avoided the blow and, taking him bodily in my arms, went out of the cafe, across the Place Victor Hugo. Not many minutes later Vincent found himself in his bed, where, in a few seconds, he was asleep, not to awaken again till morning.

"When he awoke, he said to me very calmly: 'My dear Gauguin, I have a vague memory that I offended you last evening.'

"Answer: 'I forgive you gladly and with all my heart, but yesterday's scene might occur again and if I were struck I might lose control of myself and give you a choking. So permit me to write to your brother and tell him that I am coming back.' My God, what a day!

"When evening had come and I had bolted my dinner, I felt I must go out alone and take the air along some paths that were bordered by flowering laurel. I had almost crossed the Place Victor Hugo when I heard behind me a well-known step, short, quick, irregular. I turned about on the instant as Vincent rushed toward me, an open razor in his hand. My look at that moment must have had power in it, for he stopped and, lowering his head, set off running toward home.

"Was I negligent on this occasion? Should I have

disarmed him and tried to calm him? I have often questioned my conscience about this, but I have never found
anything to reproach myself with. Let him who will,
fling the stone at me.

"With one bound I was in a good Arlesian hotel,
where, after I had enquired the time, I engaged a room
and went to bed.

"I was so agitated that I could not get to sleep
till about three in the morning, and I awoke rather late,
at about half-past seven.

"Reaching the square, I saw a great crowd collected. Near our house there were some gendarmes and
a little gentleman in a melon-shaped hat who was the
superintendent of police.

"This is what had happened.

"Van Gogh had gone back to the house and had
immediately cut off his ear close to the head. He must
have taken some time to stop the flow of blood, for the
day after there were a lot of wet towels lying about
on the flagstones in the two lower rooms. The blood had
stained the two rooms and the little stairway that led
up to our bedroom.

"When he was in a condition to go out, with his
head enveloped in a Basque *beret* which he had pulled
far down, he went straight to a certain house where for
want of a fellow-countrywoman one can pick up an
acquaintance, and gave the manager his ear, carefully
washed and placed in an envelope. 'Here is a souvenir

of me', he said. Then he ran off home, where he went to bed and to sleep. He took pains, however, to close the blinds and set a lighted lamp on a table near the window.

"Ten minutes later the whole street assigned to the *filles de joie* was in commotion and they were chattering over what had happened.

"I had no faintest suspicion of all this when I presented myself at the door of our house and the gentleman in the melon-shaped hat said to me abruptly and in a tone that was more than severe, 'What have you done to your comrade, Monsieur?' "

Gauguin relates how he succeeded in making the police know he was not responsible for Van Gogh's mutilation. He then had Vincent removed to the hospital, and set out almost immediately for Paris, never again to see his comrade of the fruitful months at Arles.

Van Gogh shortly afterwards was removed to the madhouse at Auvers, where, in flashes of lucidity, he "furiously painted the admirable pictures we know."

It was in one of these intervals of sanity that the painter, realizing his condition, went one day into the fields, seated himself under a tree, took a revolver from his pocket, and shot himself through the chest. He then arose to his feet, and wandered back to the inn of the establishment, where he calmly and in a very gentle voice announced to the attendants, who thought he had met with an accident, "I have killed myself."

He smoked his pipe while his friend Dr. Gachet, of whom he had painted a portrait, examined him, and received philosophically the doctor's report he was dying.

Van Gogh was a Hollander by birth, of date 1853. His father was pastor in the Dutch Protestant church, and the household was one of gloomy austerity. Ill-clad and poor, and of a reserved, brooding, violent temper, Vincent was an outcast among his schoolmates.

He was of a mind to follow in his father's footsteps, but his showing in his school studies was so poor the elder Van Gogh decided to make of him a salesman. A relative was in the art business, associated with The Hague branch of Goupil of Paris, and a job was secured for Vincent there.

"That or a grocery, it doesn't matter which," said his father.

It was thus, at sixteen, that Vincent was brought into intimate contact with pictures, and his destiny began to take shape.

Alfred Stevens of Brussels, one of the Impressionists — highly "modern" for the period — was a favorite with patrons of The Hague branch of Goupil's, and the paintings of Stevens helped to anchor Van Gogh's tastes. To his dying day, Van Gogh was an "Impressionist" on the surface, however violently he violated the rules in the internal structure of his volcanic, chaotic art.

After four years, Van Gogh was transferred to the London branch of Goupil's, where he came in contact with the paintings of Constable and Turner. He showed little discrimination in taste, however, for he admired, too, James Tissot, whose Holy Land pictures once set agog the Babbitts the world over. A more powerful fascination came, however, to his rescue — Millet and the Barbizon painters.

Van Gogh was proving fairly successful as a salesman and had begun to paint clumsily in imitation of the things he liked, when he fell in love, at 20, with an English girl already engaged. She refused to jilt her fiance for him, and he quit his job and went back to Holland in a state of despair that made his family fear for his reason.

A transfer to the Paris house of Goupil's was secured for him, but his picture-selling days were about over. After a few months he handed in his resignation, to the distress of his father, and went back to London, determined to study theology, aiming to support himself by teaching French.

It was his lady love, of course, that drew him across the Channel, even if he persuaded himself he had a call to a high religious mission. Her marriage shortly after his arrival in London again plunged him into the darkest despair, and he returned to Holland and the house of his father.

An uncle in Amsterdam offered to help him

through a long theological course there, and Vincent accepted. But he had read Michelet and Renan, and found his instructors stupid. Accordingly, he neglected his formal studies, but set about preaching fervid, violent sermons to peasants in districts around Amsterdam. Reports reached his professors, there were some turbulent interviews, and Vincent discontinued his course.

Van Gogh then went into the mining districts of Belgium, where he labored with zeal for the salvation of the souls of the workmen, living hungry and almost naked in a hovel. Here, however, he began in earnest a far more important work — sketching the people and the life around him. He engaged, too, in an illicit love affair, that weighed heavily on his morbid, evangelistic soul, but may have served a good purpose in pointing the way back to a secular world.

His brother Theodore, a more docile employe of Goupil's, and Vincent's devoted slave his whole life through, sent him what money he could from his own meager salary. The sale by Theodore of a few of Vincent's sketches encouraged the family, though the monetary consideration was of little consequence.

Vincent gradually began to develop an obsession he could impart the religious fervor of his soul better to his fellow-men through the medium of the brush than by his tongue, and his evangelistic zeal took a new and fortunate course.

Van Gogh painted in various localities of Belgium

VINCENT VAN GOGH   LA BERCEUSE

and Holland, copying works he admired in museums for practice, studying under this local master or that for a few weeks, developing his crude talents and sublimating his evangelism, without doing violence to the genius that was in him.

Finally, in 1886, he went to Paris, to live with his brother, Theodore. Here he came in contact with Impressionism in all its vividness, and here he went to school again for a few months to learn the technique of the new things that so dazzled him. Through a fellow student, Emile Bernard, he came in contact with Gauguin. He met, also, Toulouse-Lautrec, and, in a joint exhibition with this disciple of Daumier, he sold a few of his paintings, which raised his spirits.

He stayed in Paris fifteen months, quarreling almost incessantly with his long-suffering brother over trifles, and then, one morning, abrutly left. Theo was to be married, and Vincent got the idea he would no longer be wanted in the flat.

He went to Arles in February, 1888, where a little later he was joined by Gauguin. In the two ensuing years — he died in July, 1890 — Van Gogh did that amazing series of canvases that stamp him one of the great masters of all time. They are the psychological record of a mighty, if morbid, soul.

Gauguin's life story is no less hectic, and is more luridly picturesque. He furnished much sensational newspaper copy during his career, and has been elevated into a hero of fiction in W. Somerset Maugham's "The Moon and Sixpence". He had a decided literary skill, too, and "Noa Noa" and "Intimate Journals" are among the treasures of modern letters, of value comparable with his paintings.

The Arles sojourn, a vital factor in the life of Van Gogh, was little more than a passing incident in the career of Gauguin. It is with Tahiti and the Islands of the Pacific he is most concerned.

Gauguin was born in Paris, June 8, 1848, the son of a newspaperman from the Orleans district. It was not inheritance from his French father, however, that was to determine his career. He was the child of his mother, Aline Marie Chazal, daughter of the picturesque, gay Flora Tristan, a Peruvian who had been a political factor in Louis-Philippe's reign.

Three years after Paul's birth, the Gauguin family set sail for Peru, in the hope of mending fortunes shattered by the revolution of 1848. On the way out, the father died, and Aline Marie Chazal Gauguin returned to the scenes of her own girlhood with the baby Paul and his sister Mary. Gauguin's early days were thus spent in tropical Peru. It was the tropics that called him later in life for his great work.

Mme. Gauguin brought her children back to France when Paul was 7, and placed them in school. At 17, the future painter secured an appointment in the navy, and again went into the fated tropics on a cruise. On a second voyage, his mother died, and when Paul returned to France, a friend of his late mother got a place for him in a broker's office.

Gauguin displayed from the outset a remarkable, first-rate financial genius. He penetrated within a few months the mysteries of the stock exchange, and was so lucky in speculations on his own account that he became comparatively rich in a very short time. He married, at 25, a Danish girl, and settled down, apparently, to become one of the masters of finance of Paris.

Like many other prosperous business men — we have them in Chicago, with an organized art league — Gauguin began painting Sundays for recreation.

He struck up a friendship with Camille Pissarro, the Danish West Indian Jew, who became his instructor, just as, a couple of years earlier, he had been the instructor of Paul Cézanne. A mighty "school master'" this Pissarro, even if, in accomplishment, he was only a good second-rater.

Gauguin, also, played with sculpture on Sundays, carving out of marble small figures in the studio of his landlord, Bouillot, a sculptor.

Neither his paintings nor his sculpture, in these early days, indicated any future for Gauguin. His canvases that survive are weakly Impressionistic — of no more distinction than the paintings of the Dunes around Lake Michigan by many a member of the Business Men's Art Club of Chicago. His marbles, of which one is a portrait of his son, are good student work, after the manner of Canova.

The prosperous young broker, of this period, was just a Babbitt, flattered by his associates and by interested friends, just as are the Babbitts of the Chicago Business Men's Art Club. Pissarro introduced him around. It was a proud day for Babbitt Gauguin when the great Manet himself deigned to shake hands with him, to discuss art with him, to encourage him in his efforts. He met Cézanne, too, then one of the meanest of the tribe of rebels, and ever afterward claimed Cézanne as his friend. He, with Renoir, has the distinction of "discovering" Cézanne, despised and rejected by the rest — but the fact that Gauguin always annoyed Cézanne may be a "hangover" from the Peruvian's Babbitt days.

Gauguin, like many another Babbitt blessed with money, bought paintings from his friends — 15,000 francs' worth — no mean sum in those days. Regular buyers of pictures were laughing at the "crazy" Impressionists, and their pictures at auction were bringing at the most and very unusually a couple of hundred francs. Gauguin bought canvases by his teacher Pissarro, his distinguished friend Manet, Renoir, Guillaumin, Sisley, even the lowly Cézanne. In later years, when reverses came, Gauguin was forced to sell all these early prizes — all except a still life by Cézanne, which he idolized, and a landscape by Pissarro, which he retained through sentiment.

Gauguin was permitting his fervid Peruvian soul to dwell more and more on his painting and less and less on the stock exchange. He began exhibiting with his friends. The great Joris-Karl Huysmans, critic, singled out, in 1881, a nude of his and admired its realism even above Courbet. Such praise stunned the Babbitt soul of the broker. The making of money was becoming a frightful bore. In January, 1883, Gauguin gave up his seat on the stock exchange, determined to devote his life henceforth to painting.

The Gauguin legend, as most people have it in mind, requires that the broker desert his wife and children next morning, sail within a week for Tahiti, and sleep within another month in the arms of his brown mistress. The facts are somewhat less romantic.

The decision to sacrifice forty thousand francs a year for a mirage made no hit with the practical Mme. Gauguin, with their children growing up around them. But she was game, and stuck. They had some money laid aside, and managed to keep fed and clothed and retain some of their airs of prosperity.

Gauguin's paintings proved unsalable, however — the reason is plain, when one of them of this period is examined today, even in the mellowing glow of his later genius — and after a few months, with all their money going out and nothing coming in, they left

Paris and went to live at Rouen, where expenses were less. This change was only a temporary expedient, and eight months later, they decided to go to Denmark, where Mme. Gauguin's family might help him to a job that would pay expenses without interfering with his "art".

"Art" it must be called, in quotation marks, even that which came into being in Copenhagen. Never did a Business Men's Art-Leaguer of less apparent talent try to foist himself onto the world — even those who get their things hung in the annual shows in the Art Institute of Chicago by some mysterious telepathic communication with the juries.

In June, 1885, the Gauguins separated, after reports that Paul's Peruvian blood had not successfully resisted the blandishments of the maidens of Copenhagen. Gauguin returned to Paris, and to his friends, and in 1886 again exhibited with them. He was still trying to be an Impressionist, a lesser — far lesser — Pissarro.

He made next a trip into Brittany, where he was gripped by the long barren stretches of landscape of monotone color, and here he seems to have awakened to a sense of values of broad, flat surfaces. He was too much the student of Pissarro to apply with full assurance his observations, yet the birth of the genius of Gauguin occurred in this excursion into Brittany. Coming back to Paris, he met, through his friend Bernard, the strangely rugged painter from Holland, Vincent Van Gogh, newly arrived in the art capital. The meeting was casual.

Gauguin, restless under his poverty, and remembering the tropical adventures of his youth, persuaded an artist friend, Charles Laval, to ship with him for Martinique, where living was cheaper. They stayed there only a few months, however, for Laval fell ill, and attempted suicide.

But those few months worked magic in the soul of Gauguin. Remembering subconsciously the broad plains of Brittany, and applying the inspiration to Martinique, Gauguin took back to Paris several canvases painted with a wide brush stroke, at variance with the minute shreds, and hatchings and dots of color he had been instructed to use. His friends were not enthusiastic.

Gauguin and Van Gogh met again. Charles Laval was a physical wreck — the Martinique fever, which Gauguin's tropical blood had been able to resist, had got in its deadly work on his young friend. Van Gogh left for Arles and persuaded Gauguin to follow him.

After the episode of the severed ear — Gauguin seems to have played in hard luck with his friends, for Laval had attempted suicide in Martinique — the Peruvian came back to Paris.

It wasn't long before he was in a controversy with his friend Bernard, developing also a broad brush stroke, as to which was master and which disciple.

[111]

Gauguin, also, became involved in a dispute with
Cézanne — evidences of Cézannish influence were alleged in the new things Gauguin was doing — his famous "Yellow Christ" belongs to this period. It was
Cézanne who was annoyed, not Gauguin.

"He never understood me," said Cézanne long
afterward. "I never have and never will agree to the
absence of modelling or gradation; that is nonsense.
Gauguin is not a painter: he has only turned out fantastic figures."

(A queer parallel is discoverable in the antipathy
a great painter of antiquity had for another great
painter. Michelangelo, according to El Greco, was "a
good sort of man, but did not know how to paint.")

After other painting expeditions into Brittany, and
after lingering around Paris with no great luck, Gauguin ran across a booklet describing Tahiti. His tropical blood was stirred, he got together thirty of his paintings, auctioned them off for nearly ten thousand francs
— a fourth of what he once earned annually as a broker
— secured a vague "art commission" to Tahiti from
the government, and on April 4, 1891, set out on his
immortal journey to the paradise of the Pacific. It was
thus eight years after his giving up his seat on the stock
exchange, instead of one night, and six years after his
separation from his wife.

Gauguin's life in the tropics for the next dozen
years, with an occasional return to Paris to look after

MARC CHAGALL   LA PROMENADE

the selling of his pictures, too "wild" for his contemporaries to buy, is a long romance, with much of tragedy mingled with it.

He took a Tahitian wife, who was not faithful to him; he sank low in the estimation of the white men of the island — and of the brown; he became a savage in appearance and something of one in words and action. Scandalous stories were told of him — stories he matched with tales he told himself in "Noa Noa" and "Intimate Journals".

But, in spite of all — indeed, because of all — he painted those canvases rapidly becoming priceless, revealing not only a race, but, more important, the flaming soul of a genius. Once he had broken away from the technique of his friends, the Impressionists; once he had found a powerful, unique expression in broad brush strokes and barbaric colors arrayed against each other; once he had attuned this expression to what was in his tropical, savage soul, Paul Gauguin began to paint things that will be deathless as long as his canvases endure — things he expressed, too, in literary form, fearlessly and with fervid intensity.

His is one of the most passionate souls art has known through the ages — matching the soul of El Greco.

"Decorative", his paintings have been classified, but any implication of inferiority in the word is without justification. If his figures are "without modelling or gradation", as Cézanne charged — a charge that breaks down in presence of his later Tahitian canvases, even though they are still flatter than Cézanne's — they are so much the more in the mood of Gauguin's expression — so much the more his language — just as Cézanne's three-dimensioned solids are the language of "the primitive of the way"— just as Van Gogh's strange, elongated shreds of Impressionistic color over a solidity of form no great Dutchman has escaped since Rembrandt are the substitute for the verbal thunderings of the evangelist.

Three great geniuses, vastly at variance with each other — each a soul on fire — ushered in Expressionism.

OF AUGUSTE RENOIR
and His Dazzling Nudes

A<small>MID</small> the turmoil and the ballyhoo of the "isms" that gave the first two decades of the present century the semblance of the Midway at a World's Fair, one painter was quietly at work accomplishing a miracle.

He was Auguste Renoir, in his sixtieth year when the century dawned, who might have sat back and rested content with the laurels won as an "Impressionist"— important as any, with the single exception of Claude Monet.

But, at the period of life when the pulse is supposed to calm down, when the hot fire of youthful genius is supposed to have consumed all the resin — to cease to crackle and begin to smoulder — Renoir started upon the work that will make his name live forever in the annals of art.

While the Futurists were loudly bawling the death of the nude — or, at any rate, its abeyance for ten

years — joining with the Cubists in preaching a doctrine of complete sublimation of woman's lovely body
in the direction of the abstract — during that very
decade, Renoir was elevating the female nude to heights
of glory she had not known in the history of the world
— heights beyond the dreams of Goya, and Rubens,
and Titian, and Giorgione — beyond, probably, Apelles.

Renoir, born in 1841, only two years after
Cézanne, twelve years before Van Gogh and seven before Gauguin, nevertheless is, in his later and more significant phases, rather of the generation of Matisse and
Picasso. He was a youth of 28, with already one rejection by the Salon to his credit, when Matisse was born,
and was beginning to come into his own, a man of 40,
along with his fellow Impressionists, when Picasso
opened his infant eyes on Andalusia.

Renoir from his first association with the rebels of
Paris in the sixties, whose god was Manet, displayed a
fondness for brilliance of color beyond any of his fellows. Throughout his Impressionistic period this brilliance persisted, giving a barbaric, gem-like richness to
his landscapes, ranking them below the cooler canvases
of Claude Monet.

When, however, like his friend Cézanne, he cut
away from the leading strings of Monet, and started on
a path of his own, these same rich, jewelled colors were
found to be the exact medium he required — it is they
that gave to his nudes the sensuous fire they possess

above all the nudes of history — a sensuousness re-strained, animal and innocent in its quality — Renoir is never pornographic.

Renoir, in his sixty years as a painter, had learned, too, to put passionate fire into his drawing — it amused him to recall the many uncritical comments that had been hurled against him as being a bad drafts-man. He did a few etchings comparable with his paint-ings. At the age of 75, he even turned sculptor, pro-ducing half a dozen female nudes that rank him as high, in this art, as that other astonishing painter who took to clay, Degas. Into his etchings and his sculpture, he succeeded in injecting much of the same sort of hot vitality his color conveys, without, however, reaching its full intensity.

Renoir's passion for pure, glowing color is ascribed to his earliest art occupation, painting on porcelain for a manufacturer to whom his parents apprenticed him when a child. His passion for the nude — outside the natural instincts of a red-blooded man — was inflamed a little later by his next occupation as a painter of fans — subjects for which he found in the Louvre in the pictures by Boucher, Watteau and Lancret. It was in 1866, while making his living as a fan painter, that Renoir transferred one of his inspirations to canvas — "The Huntress Diana" — which was promptly rejected by the Salon.

This was a life-size nude — "It was intended to be

nothing more than a nude", Renoir told Vollard, who has done for him a spicy biography on a par with his "Cézanne". "But the picture was thought improper, so I put a bow in the model's hand and a doe at her feet. I added an animal skin to make it less blatantly naked, and the picture became a 'Diana'."

"The Huntress Diana" is still extant, but a more "successful" picture — so far as Salon honors go — "Esmeralda", of date 1863, is not.

"A big canvas of mine was accepted that year", Renoir related to Vollard. "Oddly enough, I was championed by Cabanel, who was chairman of the jury. Not that he cared for my work. On the contrary, he declared that he thoroly disliked it. 'But in spite of that', he hastened to add, 'it is an effort which ought to be recognized.' The canvas represented Esmeralda dancing with her goat around a fire, surrounded by a circle of beggars. I remember the reflections of the flames and the great shadows of the cathedral. After the Salon was over, I destroyed it, partly because it was too cumbersome, and partly because I had conceived a distaste for bitumen, which I had not yet discarded when it was painted. Just my luck! The same day an Englishman, who wanted that very picture, came to see me. I can honestly say that the 'Esmeralda' was the last thing I ever painted with bitumen."

This was the period when the rebellion of the progressive young painters of Paris against the historic

Salon broke out, with the establishment that year, 1863, of the *Salon des Refusés*. Renoir was a student in the studio of Gleyre, along with Monet, Sisley and Bazille. Diaz was his special god, at the moment, and Corot and Courbet strongly excited his interest. Like the other rebels, he was fascinated, too, by the spectacular young Edouard Manet. But he also clung passionately to Delacroix, with his rich Orientalism, who was beginning, even then, to grow a trifle "old-fashioned"— and to the end of his days, Renoir never quite escaped from the magic spell Delacroix had cast over his youth.

Renoir, with such associates, and with his own natural sense of freedom, was soon at outs with the Salon of Cabanel, and was ranked with the "Impressionists". While he was not regarded by his associates as being as hopeless as Cézanne, some idea of his standing may be gathered from a remark made by Edouard Manet, sage and mentor of the group, to Claude Monet.

It was shortly after Renoir had painted his immortal two little circus girls juggling oranges, now in the Potter Palmer collection in the Art Institute of Chicago. He had painted, too, the wife and children of Monet, and Manet was preparing to do this latter subject himself. Manet was a guest at Monet's house for the purpose, when Renoir dropped in by chance for a few moments. When he was gone, Manet remarked to Monet:

"You're a good friend of Renoir; you ought to advise him to give up painting. You can see yourself he hasn't the ghost of a show."

Sincere as was Renoir's enthusiasm for the Impressionists, whole-hearted as was his part in the battle in behalf of the whole group, he was never any more of an "Impressionist" of the type of Monet and Pissarro than was his friend Cézanne.

As early as 1875, Renoir painted a nude that foreshadowed the marvelous creatures of the present century — a handsome, animal girl, with heavy loins, and a placid expression, derived evidently from Ingres — from whom, however, the mature Renoir was to depart radically.

This year, too, Renoir was commissioned to copy "The Jewish Marriage" by Delacroix — and in the process of the copying, the Oriental luxuriousness of the painter of "Women of Algiers" heated by a degree or two his already feverish blood. The nude female began to supplant in him the art enthusiasm he had had along with his Impressionistic friends for the play of light on a landscape. This same play of light on a velvet body, with its sheens of silk and satin, began to take on the strength of an obsession.

In 1881, after a visit to Italy and a glimpse of Raphael's "Venus", Renoir did a "Bather", sitting down, with her hair spread over her back, a young woman who "dazzles us by the incredible brilliance of her pink and white flesh, of her golden hair, and her child-

AUGUSTE RENOIR   BAIGNEUSE ASSISE

like eyes", as Renoir's biographer and critic, François Fosca, expresses it. "There are just a few shadows — under her breast, in the fold of the groin, and under the arm — no more. The whole is bathed in a light of supernatural purity."

In 1885, he gave to the world his first version of *Les Grandes Baigneuses,* in which the individual trend of his genius is apparent. Starting this picture — about the time of Edouard Manet's death in 1883 — Renoir had come to a realization that his path lay no longer in the direction Claude Monet was going.

"A sort of break appeared in my work", he told Vollard. "I had pushed Impressionism as far as possible, and I came to the conclusion that I could neither paint nor draw. In fact, I got into a blind alley."

His brilliant exit from this "blind alley" during the remaining years of the century, with sensational markers along the road he traveled — nudes, and more nudes — becomes thrillingly evident in the magnificent second version of "Grand Bathers", which he accomplished in 1901. He had gone a long way and reached a goal no painter in history had attained.

A journey to Spain about 1890 is a significant incident in his development. Like Manet, he saw Goya and was equally delighted. Manet, however, on his return, painted "Olympia"— transforming Goya's lovely aristocratic wanton "Maja" into a Paris harlot. Renoir returned with this report:

"In front of Goya's 'Royal Family', which, by itself is worth the journey to Madrid, do you only notice that the king looks like a pork-butcher and the queen seems to have come straight out of a low cafe, to say nothing worse? No! Look at the diamonds she's smothered in! No one paints diamonds like Goya: and the little satin shoes he does for you — !"

Nevertheless, the queen who seemed "to have come straight out of a low cafe, to say nothing worse", stuck in Renoir's subconscious.

"I told the painter how delighted I had been with the two nudes in the dining-room", Vollard relates of his first visit to the home of Renoir.

"They are studies of the maids", answered the master. "Some of our servants have had admirable figures, and have posed like angels. But I must admit I'm not hard to please. I had just as lief paint the first old crock that comes along, just as long as she has skin that takes the light. I don't see how artists can paint those over-bred females they call society women! Have you ever seen a society woman whose hands were worth the painting? A woman's hands are lovely — if they are accustomed to housework. At the Farnesina in Rome there is a 'Venus Supplicating Jupiter', by Raphael. What marvelous hands and arms! She looks like a great, healthy housewife snatched for a moment from her kitchen to pose for Venus! That's why Stendhal thought that Raphael's women were common and gross."

[122]

Goya's queen, with her lustful, healthy, kitchen-wench flesh, had a rival, in Renoir's admiration, in Boucher's girls with "most enchanting little dimples" in their thighs. "It's odd", he remarked to Vollard on another occasion, "that people are never willing to give a man credit for what he can do. They say: 'I like Titian better than Boucher.' Good Lord, so do I! But that has nothing to do with the fact that Boucher painted lovely women superbly. A painter who has the feel for breasts and thighs is saved!"

Boucher's "Diana at the Bath", he informed Vollard, "was the first picture that took my fancy, and I have clung to it all my life as one does to one's first love."

In his new, passionate understanding of women as females, it was their velvety bodies and animal faces — alluring but vacantly placid — that intrigued Renoir. He cared nothing for their intellects — and this is the type he gave to the world — glorious animals — surpassing the women of Goya, of Rubens, of Titian, of Giorgione — of Apelles.

"The women whom Renoir presents to us now", remarks Fosca, in discussing the late stages in his evolution, "are no longer unclad Parisians, surprised at their toilettes, with their surroundings of furniture, peignoirs and linen. Now he paints nudes in the open air. His models know nothing of pinched shoes and painful corsets. They have always been naked, and if

[123]

they put on clothes, they will be of soft, supple stuffs, which merely flow close to them. They move in a pearly light, and their rosy flesh shimmers against the green undergrowth. The old master takes up again his theme of 'Bathers'. In one of those canvases, dated about 1897, they frolic and play as if drunk with sunshine. Then, in 1901, in a curious replica, which is to be found in the Vollard collection, he begins again the big 'Bathers' of 1885, but in an entirely different manner, weaving on his canvas an absolute network of vibrating, contrasting brush-strokes."

Renoir, like Zorn, found his favorite models among his serving maids — Zorn's best model was his cook — Renoir's a nurse maid of his children.

"Sublimated sensuality" has been offered seriously as an explanation for the tremendous "kick" of his pictures. "To paint a woman excites him more than if he were caressing her", remarked the artist Joyant, discussing Renoir with a friend. It may be of significance that his most ravishing nudes were painted after he was sixty, and when he was so crippled with the gout that he had to be wheeled in a chair, and his brush had to be tied to the back of his hand, his fingers being too nerveless to grasp and hold it.

Renoir himself never denied the "sex appeal" his models had for him.

"I started that nude with a model that Madame Frey had sent me", he told Vollard, who was examining a painting of a very fine head, with the body only sketched in, and uncompleted.

" 'I can guarantee', she wrote, 'that this young girl has a good moral character.' But when she had undressed, I could easily have dispensed with her moral character if her breasts had only been firmer! I kept that canvas for the little girl's head rather than for the nude."

Shortly after Renoir's death of pneumonia, on December 17, 1919, the painter Maurice Denis in his *Nouvelles Théories,* offered an explanation of the fact that these naked females fail to offend despite their frank sensuality:

"Why is it that his nude figures do not shock us? First of all, because they are healthy; secondly, because this is 'painting'. Renoir's lyrical feeling and plastic sense have transfigured them. They are not idealized (thank heaven!) but they have become just form and color. The world in which they display their pearl-like dimpled bodies is the world of painting: such is the magic of art that they no longer exist except as rosy light, relieved by pearly grey, lilac and green, sustained by certain harmonious volumes and balanced masses. Signs, symbols, images that they are of Renoir's optimistic sensibility, they retain nothing of Nature but what the painter has determined to retain for the joy of the spirit, and for delectation as they said in the days of Poussin — nothing at all for the lower passions.

"Besides, the type of humanity he has created, the wealth of splendid bodies, the robust architecture of these flesh and blood constructions, stamped with a feeling of classic serenity, is free from all perversity. *Sana, sancta.* Their expression of innocent animalism makes them of the same kind in the realm of nature as flowers or magnificent fruits. Never did antiquity better portray the frankness of instinct, nor in a manner at once more sensual or more chaste."

Though he went an entirely different path, Renoir's evolution out of Impressionism was influenced largely by Cézanne. He was the first of all the painter associates to scent the direction Cézanne was going, and was his staunch admirer, from the first, when Cézanne was the annoyance of his fellow Impressionists, to the last, when Cézanne had achieved his brilliant immortality — Renoir lived long enough to witness the canonization, which the "primitive of the way" pathetically missed.

It was in 1863, in a little studio he shared with Bazille, that Renoir met Cézanne. Bazille brought home one day two young men, Cézanne and Pissarro.

"I came to know both intimately later on", Renoir told Vollard, "but it was Cézanne who made the sharpest impression on my mind. I do not believe that a case like Cézanne's is to be found in the whole history of art. Think of him living to the age of 66, and, from the first day he took a brush in his hand, remaining as isolated as if he were on a desert island! And then, along with a passionate love of his art, was that strange indifference to the fate of his pictures, once they were done, even when he was lucky enough to 'realize'. Can you picture Cézanne having to wait for a purchaser to be sure of his next meal if he had not an income? Can you imagine him forcing a complacent smile for an 'amateur' who dared disparage Delacroix? And with all that, he was 'so unpractical in the ways of the world', as he used to say.

"One day I met him carrying a picture one end of which was dragging along the ground. 'There's not a cent left in the house!' he informed me. 'I'm going to try to sell this canvas. It's pretty well realized, don't you think?' (It was the famous 'Bathers' of the Caille-botte Collection — a superb thing!) A few days later I met Cézanne again.

" 'My dear Renoir', he said feelingly, 'I am so happy! I've had great success with my picture. It has been taken by someone who really likes it!'

" 'What luck!' I said to myself. 'He's found a buyer.'

"The 'buyer' was Cabaner, a poor devil of a musician, who had all he could do to earn four or five francs a day. Cézanne had met him in the street, and Cabaner went into such ecstasies over the canvas that the painter made him a present of it."

A comparison of this "Bathers" of Cézanne's — a

work as priceless as the finest Raphaels or Titians or Rembrandts — with Renoir's "Bathers" of 1901 indicates as well as any two of their pictures can do the divergence of the paths these two geniuses traveled. Cézanne's is sexless — a monumental milestone in the direction toward the "abstract" that "Modern Art" has traveled. Renoir's is sensuous — warmly human. They are supreme achievements of contemporary giants. Cézanne proved the "primitive of the way" a multitude of disciples was to travel. Renoir has had little influence on a succeeding generation.

But it may be that, in the inevitable revolt from "abstraction" — early rumbles of the revolution already are definitely heard — Renoir's magnificent nudes will prove the alluring Siren — the Lorelei. Let us devoutly pray so. Renoir will be the salvation from — Bouguereau!

GEORGES SEURAT

HENRI ROUSSEAU:

Authentic Modern "Primitive"

COMPARED to Rousseau, Cézanne is a trickster!"

Thus observed the painter Derain to the painter Vlaminck, both thorough "Moderns", and both understanding, consequently, the language that is Greek to our "critics", museum lecturers and prominent members of art clubs consulted by newspaper reporters.

If "Modern Art" is to be regarded as a true reversion to the "Primitive", then Henri-Julien Rousseau, called *"le Douanier"*, from his job as customs collector, more nearly approximates the ideal than Cézanne. If, however, "Modernism" be regarded as the "Primitive" done over — highly sophisticated — in the light of the experience of the ages, then the miserably poor customs official and teacher of the violin plays second fiddle to the son of the banker of Aix.

Rousseau, like Renoir, belongs to the present century in his real significance, though born in 1844. It was not until he was 40 that he began to paint in earnest, and his recognition was almost simultaneous with that of Matisse. It was during the last six years of his life which ended in 1910 that he did his magic jungles.

Unlike Renoir — unlike Cézanne — Rousseau was no evolution from any established "style" of art. He is the nearest product of a unique inner urge to paint that the modern movement has produced — the nearest genuine "Expressionist"— the nearest "Primitive".

Both the German critics who "discovered" Rousseau — though *le Douanier* was a Frenchman — and the Parisians who finally woke up to the fact that the "half-wit" at whom they had been poking fun was a genius, still consider him an absolutely original manifestation, without antecedents. I wish to take exception, and offer in evidence Geertgen Tot Sint-Jans, fifteenth century painter of Haarlem, with his "Nativity" in the National Gallery, London, and more especially his "St. John the Baptist" in the Berlin Gallery. In both, I believe, is a spirit closely akin to Rousseau's, and in the latter appear with strange identity the fairy trees of opiate forests.

Consideration as a source may also be given Peter Bruegel. Rousseau's peasant dance styled "The Centenary of Independence" is no mean companion piece in spirit to such things as Bruegel's "Village Wedding." Rousseau may have deliberately copied Bruegel as best he could, for, like Cézanne and Van Gogh, he did not hesitate to try to do over certain things he admired, but the resemblance is more on the surface and not of inner essence, as appears to be the case in comparison with Geertgen Tot Sint-Jans. More than one of the "Little Dutch Masters" had a way of painting leaves that resemble Rousseau's.

Rousseau was as industrious a haunter of the Louvre as was Cézanne, and despite his reputation as the prize booby and the heaven-sent butt of the Latin Quarter, his paintings, bizarre as they are, display a high technical skill. Rousseau certainly knew what he was doing with paint, and so evident was the fact to the more sensitive of his fellow artists that there was suspicion he was consciously and deliberately living up to his reputation as a fool because of the notoriety it brought him. As early as 1888, Odilon Redon, who was on the committee of the Independents of Paris, sensed something fascinating in the strange, crude work of this peasant.

For Rousseau, like Peter Bruegel, was of the people. He was born at Laval, into a family that made a living by daily toil, and for forty years he was compelled to work hard six days out of every week for enough bread to sustain him and enough cloth to cover his body. His lot was physically a little easier than that of most of his neighbors, but his job of collecting customs was as irksome and as dulling to the mentality as manual labor would have been.

During the latter of these years in the customs house, Rousseau — as Gauguin had done — devoted his Sundays to painting. But there was a vast difference.

Gauguin was a prosperous business man — a broker in Paris, earning forty thousand francs a year in operations in the short days of the stock exchange. Painting with him, as with our American Babbitts, who choose to spend Sundays with brush and easel instead of at the wheel of an automobile or aboard a yacht, was a plaything — a bid for popularity in "Bohemia", akin to the aspirations of the wealthy young men who haunt stage doors and take chorus girls on "wild parties".

With Rousseau, Sunday meant something else. It was the one day of the week he could rest from long hours of tiresome routine — the one day he could put on his "Sunday clothes", the one day he could have gone to see his "best girl" had he been of a mind to do so, the one day for picnics and parties.

It was this day, the only leisure time he had, that Rousseau devoted to painting — and his early subjects, like Bruegel's, were largely the holiday festivities of his fellow peasants. None of his associates at the customs house took his painting seriously — they laughed at his pictures, as Paris later was to laugh at them, and they tapped their foreheads and winked, almost without concealing from him the gesture, as Paris later was to do.

At 40, Rousseau, believing in his destiny as a painter despite the opinions of his friends, resigned his customs position, and went to a poor quarter of Paris to live. His pictures, of course, he found unsalable, and he was compelled to give violin lessons for sustenance. It is recorded, too, in the meager biographical data that have been collected, that he had two students of drawing, one 72 and the other 80 years old. His violin pupils were from families of workers, who lived in his own neighborhood, almost as poor as himself, and his fees consequently were small.

Besides being a painter, a violinist and a piano player, Rousseau was something of a poet and a composer — all his art manifestations being about on a par, in the estimate of his associates. He was self-tutored in them all.

The reputation of this queer peasant got noised about in Bohemian circles of Paris, and the "intellectuals", including the critic Guillaume Apollinaire, began to flock to his studio to enjoy a sport they could find nowhere else in Paris.

Rousseau, apparently, took their visits quite seriously, and later began to issue invitations to the more celebrated of his guests, decorated with drawings of his own. On these special evenings, he would play for his visitors, on piano or violin, music of his own composition, chanting to this accompaniment his poems. He also had made up an orchestra of his pupils, and these he led in the playing of his more elaborate musical masterpieces. Paintings of his always adorned the walls of his studio, and visitors often took away a canvas as a "souvenir". Maybe the good-natured "imbecile", who furnished the slummers with so much amusement, had a certain amount of peasant shrewdness in his madness.

Even so, the light-hearted buyers of the queer "souvenirs" put it over on the crafty peasant. For those paintings now are as eagerly sought for museums and great private collections as are those other "souvenirs" bought at the queer little shop in Paris of Père Tanguy — the apples of Paul Cézanne.

Rousseau began to exhibit regularly with the Independents, but the powers in the organization welcomed him no more effusively than the Impressionists twenty years before had welcomed Cézanne. They so manoeuvered that his pictures should be obscurely hung in the lower recesses of their galleries, but even here they were hunted out for mockery by the "wise" among the visitors. This was his almost invariable fate from 1886, when he first exhibited, until 1910, the year of his death.

Rousseau seems to have been as impervious to this ridicule and mockery of the populace as he was to that of the visitors to his studio. These annual shows were the great event in his life. He would deliver his pictures himself, wheeling them through the streets of Paris in a handcart.

Rousseau was married twice, and his third attempt, at 66, to take a blushing bride of 54, is the classic story among the cruel practical jokes his "friends" were in the habit of playing on him.

This third charmer was a maiden lady, who, despite her rather mature years, was still under the dominance of her father. He sternly forbade the marriage, having investigated Rousseau's worldly prospects and concluded his Leonie was better off where she was, a clerk in a bazaar.

Rousseau called her his "poor little one", and every day he walked nearly across Paris to take her to lunch, saving tramfare at the expense of bleeding feet. Leonie seems to have been somewhat flattered by this attention, despite the fact she could not find it in her heart to love him passionately — and besides there were suggestions that she would be the heiress of his works — an unknown quantity.

Things might have gone on indefinitely had not "friends" stepped in and reported to Rousseau that the coy Leonie had accepted him at last and had set the day. Rousseau went happily to the church, but Leonie did not show up. The poor, half-demented painter then wandered around the streets of Paris for days, lamenting his hard fate to anyone who would listen — to the intense amusement of the "practical jokers".

It was to Clemence, his first wife, that Rousseau dedicated most of his poetry — the poetry he set to music and sang for the visitors to his studio. Josephine, his second wife, seems to have been at outs with his muse. But he had a Polish young lady, Yadwiga, whose name he celebrated in song, but whose exact relationship with him has not been cleared up.

While he sold a picture now and then, and while he continued to give both piano and violin lessons, Rousseau's fortunes never materially improved.

"Want of care and comfort", relates a biographer, Roche Grey, "brought him humbly prostrate to a hospital bed. Here he passed away, qualified as an alcoholic patient, and was buried immediately in a common grave. The care of some friends, too poor or too canny to meet a more serious expense, removed his body to a tomb rented for thirty years."

That was in 1910. In only half of the thirty years his body has been lying in its rented tomb, any one of his larger canvases has so leaped in value that a fancy grave could be bought for him eternally — or leased to the day when Gabriel shall blow his horn, and the poor foolish peasant shall rise up and accompany the celestial choir on his rented violin — for he was too poor ever to pay for even the rickety instrument that helped him earn his daily bread.

Such are about all the significant facts that have been preserved concerning this strangest of all phenomena the Modernistic movement has brought forth.

There is a tradition that in his youth Rousseau went out to Mexico to fight in behalf of the Emperor Maximilian, but the story is considered improbable, and is

THE JUNGLE

HENRI ROUSSEAU

dismissed as a legend invented to account for the luxuriant tropical jungles that made their appearance about 1904, and continued until his death. It is argued that such vivid memories of the fairyland he visited in youth would not have lain dormant in a mind like his through a period of forty years.

In view of the powerful and persistent fascination the tropical vision asserted over him when it did appear, a more immediate origin is sought. It is probable this tropical glory burst upon him as a result of his visits on Sundays, in the latter years of his life when halting footsteps prevented his roaming, as of old, through the countryside, to the Jardin des Plantes in Paris. There he saw, in the hothouses, all the luxuriance of the tropics — and this more ordered vegetation resembles more the Rousseau conceptions than do the wild, disordered, matted growths of the real jungles. His jungle scenes are highly organized and highly artificial.

Rousseau's art is "Primitive" in that it came out of an untutored, crude, peasant mind — a mind that may not have been imbecile, as his contemporaries suspected, but that was certainly subnormal so far as ordered intelligence is concerned.

It is just as certain that Rousseau was not a "faker". He tried hard to draw like the academic masters — Bouguereau, who kept Cézanne out of the Salon, Rousseau regarded as the greatest artist that ever lived, and he was a passionate admirer, too, of Cabanel.

He haunted the Louvre and the Luxembourg, where he not only painstakingly studied the methods of painting and drawing in whatever he saw that entranced him, but picked up odds and ends of landscapes — little striking features he attempted to copy into his own canvases. That he was a "Primitive" from a genuine urge in his subconscious is indicated by the fact that, despite all his efforts to imitate his idols, his work maintains a very strong unity — the most amazing individuality of any painter in modern times.

His occasional suggestion of Bruegel may come more directly out of his peasant soul than from a burning desire to imitate — a kinship of peasant with peasant — for Bruegel offers insurmountable difficulties to a copyist in comparison with Bouguereau. His still more striking similarity to Geertgen Tot Sint-Jans may be due to some such common soul impulse as makes a Corsican Napoleon a counterpart of a Greek Alexander — an American Brigham Young a counterpart of a Jewish Moses — after the lapse of long centuries.

Rousseau looked at everything around him and tried to record photographically what he saw. But a strange and powerful "temperament" intervened. Some of his critics have expressed the opinion that his finished canvases are the visualization of dreams of fairyland by a mind that never attained maturity — a child mind

— a "moron". But those who are more sensitive see in his work the naivete of the African sculptors — quite a different manifestation — a full maturity in a primitive state of development.

Odilon Redon was right when he sensed back in 1888 a strange fascination he could not quite grasp.

OUT OF THE WOMB OF TIME – ONE WOMAN PAINTER

NOT the least of the triumphs of "Modern Art"— of Expressionism that defiantly asserts its right to express what is in the individual soul regardless of the scowls of the Academy — has been the production of one woman artist, the first and only painter in history who rings true as a thoroughly feminine creature.

Marie Laurencin learned her art from men — Picasso and Botticelli are clearly indicated in her evolution — but in its final sublimation, the male element is eliminated as surely as from the poetry of Sappho, with whom she has been compared by more than one sensitive critic.

Women painters, like women poets, women novelists, women musicians, women politicians, women poisoners, have been lesser men. They have gone far in imitation, but have not had the initiative or the ability to blaze new paths for themselves. The exception is the actress. On the stage it is exhibitionism dictated by vanity that counts. The woman has an enormous advantage. The quality that makes the actress is apt to wreck the actor.

Until Marie Laurencin appeared, femininity had been gallantly ascribed in France, in generous measure, to Vigee LeBrun first and then to Berthe Morisot. They undoubtedly had a fine feminine touch.

Time has practically eliminated the charming Vigee LeBrun from consideration. As the lively scandals that kept her in the public eye like another Ninon have evaporated, it has been found that the "genius" of the little LeBrun was largely of the substance of the scandals — her reputation as a painter vanished along with her notoriety. The glory of the charming French Aspasia survived only a little while the glory of the court of her patron and friend, Marie Antoinette. Her "feminine touch," consequently, ceases to be of importance as her art ceases to be of consequence. It was just a surface gloss at best. She painted more delicately than most men — less delicately than a few. But there was no material difference in basic substance.

Berthe Morisot was of a talent immeasurably superior — a talent that lies within the borderland of genius. But Mlle. Morisot, as has been pointed out, is only a lesser Manet. Her "feminine touch" sinks deeper than LeBrun's, but it does not reach the vital structure — the bone and marrow of Morisot's art is Manet.

Mary Cassatt, that other fine Impressionist, is less feminine than Berthe Morisot, despite her fondness for painting children — a fondness that amounts to an obsession in her lonely, virgin heart. Mary Cassatt's stroke is almost challengingly masculine. Had she signed her canvases just "Cassatt", the name "Mary" would have suggested itself less often to the beholder than the name "John".

Like the vast majority of women artists, Miss Cassatt preferred to be a lesser man — or the choice was forced upon her involuntarily by inner impulses. Even in the quality of tenderness, her little children — naked or half-naked girl babies — are not distinctively of feminine origin. Picasso has surpassed her, in this respect, and Daumier has equalled her.

It may be observed, incidentally, that the Impressionist Pissarro displayed often a delicacy that matches even Berthe Morisot's — this father of a whole house full of hungry children he strove valiantly to feed.

The absence of any distinctively feminine artists before Marie Laurencin cannot be laid to scarcity of female workers in paint. Since the Renaissance, they have been liberally represented in all schools and all movements. Their ideal, however, has been largely that of Rosa Bonheur — as close an approximation to man as possible. The majority of them have not gone so far as the vigorous painter of "The Horse Fair" and donned trousers, but witness the warrior maiden Onorata, decorator of the Palace at Cremona, who was fond of putting on male armor and dashing into battle. And there was Marietta, the accomplished daughter of Tintoretto, who accompanied him dressed as a boy, and was far from being the least talented of his disciples.

Toward the middle of the last century, Mrs. E. F. Ellet gathered together with great industry data of about 600 artists of her sex and published a volume entitled "Women Painters"— the most thorough and exhaustive work that has ever been done on the subject. Out of the 600, not one painter is revealed as of the first rank — nor of the fifth. Not one, so far as can be gathered from the very explicit data — set out favorably, but not unpardonably so — had ever painted a picture a man could not have done better. And no one, except Marie Laurencin, has appeared since to break the monotony.

Marie Laurencin, it may be stated at the outset, is not recognized unquestionably as a genius — or even as an artist of first importance — by some of the best friends of the modern movement. Her delicacy is rated by some of these critics as mere triviality, while her little feminine whimsicalities are frowned upon as being beneath the dignity of great art. Investigation, however, of the critics themselves usually results in the discovery of an ego that is annoyed at anything savoring of playfulness in its august presence — and the poor little Laurencin is made to stand in a corner for her naughty irreverence.

Her whimsicalities are of the essence of her art, and they cannot be denied her any more than they can be denied Sir James M. Barrie or Anatole France. Just because Cézanne never smiled, there is no reason why his disciples must maintain a long face. One of them, even, breaks into hellish laughter without losing caste — Georg Grosz.

Marie Laurencin's advent has been possible only because Expressionism is operating. In any age of the world into which she had happened to be born she would have been a good painter, but there is nothing in the nature of her art to indicate a violent revolutionist. Without the unshackling of genius, in general — the insistence of the right of even so lowly a creature as a woman to express what is in her soul — she could scarcely have developed into the lovely, exotic painter of fairy creatures too good for any realm of the imagination except the fabled Lesbos. Not that they are tainted creatures — any more than the gossamer beings who glide through the poetry of Sappho are tainted. They are purely feminine girls — daughters of Eve before she fed Adam the apple.

Marie Laurencin became a pupil, about the time

MARIE LAURENCIN   YOUNG GIRL

she was passing out of her teens, of Picasso — not much older — then in his "blue period", when Botticelli was a major influence over his daydreams. She followed Picasso enthusiastically — and his friend Braque — into their Cubistic experiments. But, though she was classed a Cubist in the first literature of the movement, she never was one genuinely, seeking beauty in abstract design. Her little feathery, fairy feminine creatures were in the habit of peeping out from behind the bars formed by the lines and angles she dutifully drew.

Gradually she eliminated Picasso from her conception of beauty — more gradually Botticelli. Her lovely creatures emerged — sometimes without noses, but never without elfin charm. Sometimes they are woodland fays, playing with strange beasts that haunt Fairyland forests — sometimes mischievous pixies of the moorlands. They are not the fairies children dream of, however. They are fairies for grown-ups, as tantalizingly sophisticated as they are femininely lovely, and slyly elusive. They are fairies with everything in their makeup women have acquired since Eden — goddesses Swinburne might have invented had he chosen to do over Homer.

Mlle. Laurencin was born in Paris in 1885. Her earliest education was in the *Lyceé Lamartine* and then with F. Humbert of the Institute. Thus grounded in the fundamentals she luckily was of age still impressionable when pandemonium broke loose in Paris with the howling of the *Fauves*. Had she not come at so early a period under the influence of Picasso and Braque, the chances are she would have developed into just another "female artist", traveling contented the well-beaten paths.

Association with the Independents of Paris has been interrupted by sojourns in Spain and Germany, which have contributed to a highly individualized art that has been progressing steadily from about 1908, when a "Girl with Flowers" began to indicate its tendency.

It was not, however, until about 1914, when "Two Sisters" was produced, that the decisive feminine element came into the ascendant. "The Clowness" of that year — she, like Renoir, and Picasso and Lautrec, has been under the spell of the circus — shows even more decidedly this exclusive femininity — a "clowness" impossible for the genius even of a Picasso. By 1918 or '19 she had reached her full development — a maturity that shows no decline in its vigor.

While not of the importance perhaps of Matisse or Picasso, Marie Laurencin is, like them, a refreshing individuality. Like Rousseau, the "Primitive", she has genius sufficient to overbalance a suggestion of "freakishness." Even as late as 1930, a woman is a "freak" if she accomplishes something a little out of the ordinary.

Suzanne Valadon is another female figure that looms large in the art circles of contemporary Paris. She is nearly a score of years older than Marie Laurencin

— her famous son, Maurice Utrillo, was born two years before Mme. Laurencin — 1883, the year Manet died.

Born in 1867, Suzanne Valadon came first into the art life of Paris as a model — a very pretty girl in her early teens. Lautrec and Degas made use of her, and it was Lautrec, who lived in the same rooming house she did, who discovered she was sketching as well as posing. He insisted on seeing her work, was impressed by it, and did much to encourage her in her ambitions. Lautrec's influence has made itself evident often in her work — as late as 1920 she did a family group strongly suggestive of his style.

It was in these first days in Paris as a model and learning to paint, that her son Utrillo was born. In this very busy early life of hers, too, she was, for a time, a circus or vaudeville performer, and she has since done harlequins and other player folk of vivid intensity.

Female nudes, however, are the most striking of all subjects to her fancy, and she does them with a male gusto. She has nothing of the feminine delicacy of a Laurencin. She chooses to compete with men on grounds where she has numerous superiors — Renoir, Picasso, Matisse, Othon Friesz, Foujita. She is decidedly of the lesser "Moderns", but of accomplishment so important that she would still be of distinction even if she were not a woman.

A youngster who has been making a noise in Paris, but whose claims to be considered a real artist are even

[147]

more harshly attacked than those of Marie Laurencin, is Helene Perdriat — a "best seller".

Mlle. Perdriat, still in her twenties, is from Brittany, horribly sophisticated, more Parisian than the Latin Quarter. Like Marie Laurencin, she has the sense of humor that damns its possessor — but the similarity stops there. The little Perdriat has not yet attained the cool, assured, sustained conviction that belongs to Laurencin — she has not demonstrated that exclusive femininity her more famous rival possesses.

Eyes are the chief obsession of Helene Perdriat — when Homer referred to Juno as "ox-eyed" he may have been prophesying the creatures the young Breton would create. Great, almond-shaped opiate eyes haunt her dream world. They are not the enigmatic slant eyes of the yellow Oriental, nor the staring, hypnotic Egyptian eyes on the coffin lids taken from the city of the dead along the Nile. They are more akin to the big, limpid eyes of Homer's heroine-villainess — but not quite hers, either. They are soft, fantastic eyes of lotus-eaters in some fabled realm of Helene's own imagination.

All of her creatures have them — not only her girls, with whom she chiefly concerns herself — and, like Laurencin's, all her girls are self-portraits — but also her dogs and her does, strange, elongated fantastic animals akin to Marc Chagall's, but even gentler, with which she peoples her forests.

[148]

Her girls are not fairies, like Laurencin's, but rather flesh and blood inhabitants of some forest of Arden — high-born damsels disguised as milkmaids, virgin but ardent. Her nudes are guileless — but bear watching. One, vividly remembered, is typical. Mlle. Perdriat has smashed against the middle of this girl a great circular plaque of flowers — without reason, without sense, without support — of more incredible impudence than the hand of the Venus de Medici or Manet's "Olympia", hiding yet indicating nudities that allure. This lovely creature, strayed out of Eden, is all the more enticing because of her great, drooping, uncomprehending eyes — eyes of the lotus-eater — Eve before the fall.

Gaudy and fantastic are Perdriat's colors, in oil and water. Strange and heathenish are her patterns. She has taken something from the late Egyptian artists working in the days of the Romans at Alexandria, and made it her own. Perhaps there is a touch of the Japanese — not the pure Oriental, but as modified by the Parisian "Moderns". But there is more of a barbarianism running wild, tossed exultantly into the canvas by the daring little Breton, who knows she is "cute" and takes advantage of it.

Mlle. Perdriat does not seem to have mastered, as yet, her art — to have curbed its exuberance — to have ordered it into a desired channel by an assured technique. But then she is young, and full of the joy of life. She moves in a highly sophisticated Bohemian circle of

Paris — the most sophisticated among her associates, and their darling. Her skill at making up her face provokes even more amused astonishment than what she puts on her canvases. She blots out her lips and eyebrows, eliminates all natural features as nearly as possible, and then proceeds to paint a face more to her liking.

THE
PARIS
PANORAMA

T HE "Modern" movement is much too young to fix
with any degree of certainty the relative standing of its
masters.

There can be little question that Cézanne is one of
the great painters of all time. He has receded far enough
into the background so that a full perspective can be
had, and he appears of the stature of Rembrandt, El
Greco, Michelangelo and Giotto. Just now he dominates
painting, but even if he should be dethroned as mentor,
and painting should take entirely a new trend, his own
superiority as an individual genius would remain. Nobody paints any more like Rembrandt, or El Greco, or
Michelangelo — certainly not like Giotto. Yet, that does
not make them any the less great.

Van Gogh and Gauguin, too, are established, but
the full measure of their genius remains to be deter-

mined. Clive Bell, for one, doubts the importance most other critics attribute to Van Gogh.

Future historians may discover that Daumier, and not Manet, was the great connecting link between Goya and Cézanne.

Degas, in his day, was esteemed above Daumier, but now he appears decidedly less. Toulouse-Lautrec may eventually, too, pass Degas in critical estimation, and rank second only to Daumier, in that line of development of "Modernism"— which may be proven, eventually, to be the correct line of descent instead of the one I have endeavored to trace, namely, through the "Impressionists".

Toulouse-Lautrec, certainly, was the superior of Degas in individual portraiture, though Degas may have been his master in fixing types.

The ballet girl of Degas — not the airy, ethereal creature you see on the stage, but the weary, heavy-footed female of tired flesh and blood, slave to the lust of audiences for all there is in a female body, is a masterwork of all time. Degas demonstrated her kinship — her identity — with the washerwoman.

But Degas never matched Toulouse-Lautrec's "La Goulue" of the Moulin Rouge, and several of those others of "the crew of repulsive night birds in old Montmartre before the foreign invasion destroyed its native and spontaneous wickedness", as Huneker expresses it.

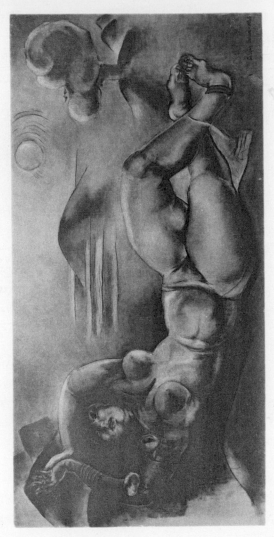

SALCIA BAHNC

These "Modernists" all are dead — long dead — the half century mark is gradually approaching.

Of the living, Matisse and Picasso seem fairly sure of immortality. Certainly they have a prominent place in art history as the arch-rebels who instigated important movements. As painters, they seem to have the vitality of genius that does not perish from the earth.

But there are others who may eventually be ranked with these and with the greatest — from among the number, future generations may even single out one as a superior master, just as we are beginning to know now that Seurat, once lightly regarded as a playboy with his little dots of *Pointillisme,* possessed a genius comparable with that of Van Gogh and Gauguin and Renoir, if not with Cézanne's own.

Attention of these future generations of critics is drawn respectfully to Georges Rouault, Amédée Modigliani, Marc Chagall, and Maurice Utrillo — Andre Derain's name is omitted, because his up-and-doing friends already have a sufficiently powerful spotlight directed on him.

Derain is easily the leader of young France in Paris today—so easily that the fact has aroused suspicion in more than one critical breast. Clive Bell's guess may be right — Derain represents what is wholly French — in America, we might call him a "hundred percenter". It is only fair to quote Mr. Bell's opinion at length:

"Derain is now the greatest power amongst young

[153]

French painters. I would like to lay stress on the words 'power' and 'French', because I do not wish to say, what may nevertheless be true, that Derain is the greatest painter in France, or seemingly to forget that Picasso's is the paramount influence in Europe. For all their abjurations most of the younger and more intelligent foreigners, within and without the gates of Paris, know well enough that Picasso is still their animator. Wherever a trace of Cubism or of *tête-de-nègre,* or of that thin, anxious line of the 'blue period' is still to be found, there the ferment of his unique spirit is at work. And I believe it is in revolt against, perhaps in terror of, this profoundly un-French spirit that the younger Frenchmen are seeking shelter and grace under the vast though unconscious nationalism of Derain."

Mr. Bell chooses to rest on the one item of Picassoism, the invention of a Spaniard, but the case is a lot bigger than that. "Modernism" is international — the most amazing pot-pourri that has been mixed in the history of the world. Cézanne was largely Italian, as was that other great Frenchman, Napoleon. His master, Pissarro, was a Portuguese Jew. Van Gogh was a Dutchman. Manet, a Frenchman, nevertheless drew most of his inspiration from the Spaniard Goya. Gauguin, partly French, was swayed almost exclusively by his tropical blood — Peruvian, with a mixture of Indian. Matisse, another Frenchman, went, like Manet, abroad for his inspiration — Persia and the Orient. Monet imported ideas and technique from England — Turner and Constable. Picasso brought to Paris not only his Spanish and Moorish backgrounds, but found extra fuel for his genius in Negro sculpture.

As if this were not enough of a mish-mash, there has been added, of late years, another ingredient which may have converted it into a "hell-broth" in the estimation of young Frenchmen whose fathers have not forgotten about the Dreyfus case. The blood of Pissarro doesn't count, but the Italian Jew, Modigliani, who became so powerful a factor in the circle of Paris youngsters before his recent death, that his spirit is still "carrying on", seems to be resented. Ask any young student returned from the purely French ateliers, and you will get a not very high opinion of Modigliani, who, nevertheless, possessed a genius of hotter fire than Derain's. The Jewish element, too, has come into "Modernism" through the Russian, Marc Chagall, of Berlin and Paris — the Russian painters find little to encourage them to try to live under native government.

Derain has not shunned the experimenting of the other lively painters of Paris. He has gone through the various phases, including even Cubism, but he emerges — a disciple of Cézanne. He is the one painter, if there is any in Paris, entitled to wear the purple mantle — even though he fails to measure up to Cézanne. But then, few who wear the ring of St. Peter have claimed equality with the first Pope for zeal.

Derain has expurgated from his art practically everything that has been tried experimentally since the "primitive of the way" laid down the brush. He is not, by any means, a slavish imitator of Cézanne — he has a quality that is distinctively "Derain"— but he builds on the solid foundation of Cézanne, who, despite his Italian ancestry, went to Poussin and Chardin principally for inspiration.

In one of his excursions away from Cézanne, Derain did a remarkable "Last Supper". Here he exhibits a spirit of the primitive comparable with Gauguin's when he painted his sensational "Yellow Christ". These are, perhaps, the two strongest religious canvases the "Modern" movement — which concerns itself rarely with sacred subjects — has produced.

Derain, having purged his art of all "international" heresy, stands forth today as the ideal Frenchman Clive Bell pictures him. However, he generally leaves the observer calm and cool. That, at least, has been my personal experience. His "Last Supper" is the only picture I have ever seen of his that electrified me as does a Cézanne or a Renoir. One landscape by Cézanne has in it more dynamite than a whole gallery of landscapes by the very able painter wearing his mantle.

Georges Rouault is the victim of some mysterious circumstance that has side-tracked — maybe only temporarily — his powerful art, so simply expressed. It is possible he is too much in the tradition of Daumier,

Degas and Lautrec — that "left hand" line, which may be, as we have already uneasily indicated, the line, after all, of legitimate descent into "Modernism", with "Impressionism" as the triumphant bastard.

At any rate, Rouault, who is one of the older of the "Moderns"— he was born in 1871, only two years after Matisse — has never had much popular recognition, though artists are well aware of his strength. Rouault, too, has a sense of humor, which is sardonic, hellish, and of deep bass in its laughter — a laugh like that is always disconcerting, and you invite a man who indulges in it to your house as seldom as possible. His "Little Olympia", with her heavy dark body, her negroid features and giant teeth, make you want to pick up tenderly Manet's pretty harlot and carry her out of such vulgar company. As you go out, you're apt to hear behind you Georges Rouault's deep "Ho! Ho!"— whereat you blush crimson, remembering the morals of the fragile creature clinging around your neck.

Modigliani, too, has done an "Olympia"— she's anybody's property, this creature of the streets — Gauguin once made her a Tahitian.

Modigliani's hot nude may be ranked ultimately with the great ones of all time — with Giorgione's "Sleeping Venus", Titian's "Venus Awake", Goya's "Maja" (nude and even more impudently clothed), with Manet's sensational wanton in the Louvre. Universal judgment is scarcely ready yet, however, for the "distorted" female, with greatly elongated torso, monster eyes and lengthened face — yet, withal, possessing a fascinating loveliness, that is a reminder of Botticelli. Entirely different females by Marie Laurencin, too, hark back to Botticelli.

Modigliani is only recently dead — a tragedy of Montmartre. He lived and loved as feverishly as he painted, conscious of his genius, ill-paid, worse fed, center of a lively group that accepted Henri Murger as philosopher — getting everything that was to be got out of "Bohemia".

Modigliani was an Italian, born in 1884, and dead in Paris at the age of 36. A girl, reputed his mistress, jumped from an upper story a few hours later, and killed herself. He brought to Paris as vivid memories of Italy as Picasso's of Spain. An artist to his finger tips, Modigliani possessed that marvelous taste the Italians have never lost, however the glory of their art has faded since the twilight of Tiepolo. He had the adroit skill that has not been lost to the nation of Botticelli and Raphael. But he had, in addition, a hot Orientalism resident in the mixture of Hebrew blood that flowed through his Italian veins.

Only a little younger than Picasso, the rebel stir in Paris incited him to something equally creative, equally individual — which does not appear, however, at this close range to have been of equal importance. His creations, however, are of such feverish sensuousness, and so morbidly entrancing that they are commended to the future generations with even more confidence than Rouault's. Modigliani never laughed.

Modigliani left a following that is a fairly well-defined group. His friend, Moise Kisling, who did a death mask, has been careful of his memory, though Kisling's art is of a different type, and of late another friend, Soutine, still more widely at variance, seems to have assumed leadership of the group. Though not of the type of Modigliani — Soutine leans toward German Expressionism — this group keeps fairly well together in the great Italian's name, and it is one of the elements that do not bow to the authority of Andre Derain.

Marc Chagall has been an easy target for those critics who see only lunacy in the aims of "Modernism". Chagall's sole unpardonable sin, however, is that he refuses to be bound by the laws of gravitation. Otherwise, he is not "wild" like the Cubists and the Futurists. He distorts and mangles, but the fragments are always recognizable.

Chagall, despite his apparent soberness, is laughing a part of the time, which makes the joke all the better. His humor is confined largely to his folk and fairy phantasies, however, and he violates the laws of gravitation quite as seriously as he does playfully.

Chagall is as "childishly naive" in painting as Swinburne is in writing his miracle play "The Masque of Queen Bersabe", in which the soldiers of King David of Israel call upon Mohammed and St. Paul to witness their oaths — as "childishly naive" as the Flemish Primitive who painted an Annunciation with a Crucifix hanging on the wall. It is conceivable that a child may take delight in Chagall just as it may in "Gulliver's Travels"— but to get the real zest of Gulliver you must have reached long ago the age when you put away childish things.

Chagall is a tremendous colorist. A gallery full of his things is overwhelming — it makes the blood rush to your head and sing in your ears. He is a powerful designer, too, and the smile that comes at first to your lips when you note a young man walking along, holding his lady love upside down high in the air with one hand, or an old man nonchalantly stepping over a house with his body at an angle of forty-five degrees, or a milkmaid going about her business with her severed head following her a yard or two behind, soon vanishes in astonishment at the rational balance of lines and planes.

Ghetto types he has done as no contemporary painter. The intensity he gets here from distortion and from clashing color is unlike anything in "Modernism". Yet, there is no apparent straining for effect, as is too often the case with the Cubists and the Futurists. Chagall gives the impression, despite his wild riots of color and distortion, of having a great reserve force —

JOAN MIRO

of having done what is vividly spread before you with great ease.

Of all the "wild men" who have gone to the extremes of "lunacy", Chagall is the most convincing emotionally.

Maurice Utrillo, son of Suzanne Valadon, performs the miracle of making houses along a village street as exciting as human faces. He has done scores of them, not only dwellings, but churches and stores and public buildings — so many that he has slipped into a formula, and his houses threaten to become as tedious as Corot's trees. His village streets have the sensational distinction of Corot's forests. His work is characterized by a simplicity that is almost primitive — indeed Utrillo is sometimes classified along with Rousseau, but the classification will not hold. Utrillo paints what he sees with great fidelity, though with drastic simplification, while Rousseau translated and transposed everything into a key of fantastic imagination. Utrillo's love for bricks and mortar amounts almost to an obsession. The suburbs of Paris have for him the magnetic appeal Notre Dame and the Madeleine and the Opera House have had for the generality of artists charmed by the present-day aspects of the capital.

Another painter who has weakened a very vivid first impression is Maurice de Vlaminck, wielder of the most intensely vivid colors that are being put on canvas. He does landscapes mostly, even more drastically simplified in their drawing than Utrillo's houses, but colored to a vividness that fairly flashes. He uses dark greens and reds, largely, but they are as if burnished. The effect is sombre, rather than happy — thunder clouds outrank his blue skies. A few Vlamincks are tremendously effective. He has developed, however, something dangerously near a formula, and while he does not exactly duplicate, he fails to vary enough to overcome an impression of sameness, all the more noticeable because his art is so strikingly individual. Vlaminck, like Rouault, is a veteran — he was born in 1876.

Othon Friesz is another of the painters to be ranked among the pioneers. He was born in Havre, in 1879. The reputation of Friesz, like that of Rouault, is less than his achievement would indicate. But his reputation, it would seem, is growing steadily, if slowly. Friesz is credited with an intellect superior to that of most of his associates in the "Modern Movement". It may be that this intellect is what stands in the way of great emotional achievement. There is no hard and fast rule. Picasso is brilliantly brainy — Cézanne was not. Leonardo da Vinci was one of the great thinkers of all time — the Douanier Rousseau was not far removed from the imbecile. The dynamic power of superior genius can manifest itself with or without the aid of superior intellect. Lesser genius is apt to find brains burdensome. This may be the case with Friesz. His work displays genuine spontaneity, but, like Derain's, it leaves the beholder cool. Friesz, at times, especially in his treatment of nudes, suggests a Teutonic heaviness. He is a "decorator" in the designing of "pattern", but does not paint "flat".

Dunoyer de Segonzac made a noise for a time, and looked like a very great painter about to "realize". He puts his paint on the canvas in great gobs and smears, with a heavy, muddy effect, but out of the mud there usually emerges a still life or a female nude of great hypnotic charm. It is a studio story that so heavy is Dunoyer's paint that one of his standing nudes, hung in an exhibition while not yet quite dry, grew tired and sat down in a corner of the frame. It is necessary to put unusually long distance between yourself and a Segonzac painting to grasp the picture emerging from the mass of sombre color. Queerly enough, his line, in his black and white drawings, is unusually delicate. There is a parallel here with Cézanne, whose water colors are evanescent, almost vaporous, in marked contrast with his massive, solid oils. The last has not been heard of Segonzac. He is still young, just turned forty. He was in the camouflage squad during the World War.

Luc-Albert Moreau has a certain kinship with Segonzac, though his work is of less intensity.

Pierre Bonnard and Albert Marquet are two of the older Independents, both superior artists, who just missed a visitation of the divine fire that struck Picasso and Matisse. Matisse owes a great deal to Marquet, a pioneer in the way the greater painter was destined to travel, but whose accomplishments fell short of genius. Bonnard, a fine painter, bears some such relation to the "Moderns" as Fantin-Latour did to the "Impressionists"— his soul with the revolutionists, but his hand holding him a little back. In the readjustment of values that is bound to come with the passing of years, Bonnard may attain the high rank among the "Moderns" his friends claim for him now.

Among the Cubists were a number of painters of high talent who were not quite of the stature of Picasso, Braque and Leger. Marcel Duchamp was one of these — painter of the famous "Nude Descending the Stairs", which was the sensation of the Armory show, when extreme "Modernism" was introduced to America. Juan Gris is another, a fellow countryman of Picasso, a vivid colorist, and who persists to this day in the Cubist "heresy". Albert Gleizes was one of the most talented, and there was Francis Picabia, adroit draftsman, who afterward became one of the leaders of "Dadaism". Metzinger and Delaunay were other names to conjure with when Cubism was a reigning sensation.

Jean Marchand is another painter who, like Derain, has been through the various phases of "Modernism" and settled down finally to paint 100 percent French. He was born the year of Utrillo, 1883. Others of that generation who have raised their heads above the forty thousand artists constituting the struggling multitude of Paris are Jean Puy, Pierre Laprade, Jules Flandrin, Pierre Girieud — and the list might be extended to cover the three or four scores of names that constitute the roll of honor Gustave Coquiot prints at the finish of his noteworthy book, *Les Indépendants*.

Younger men are coming along clamoring to be heard. There is Pruna, for example, a fellow countryman of Picasso — a disciple of Picasso — and, so far, little more than an echo of Picasso. But then, he is still in his twenties, and may develop — though Picasso, at his age, was a master.

Then there's Marcel Gromaire, just turned thirty, who appears to have something substantial as a basis. He goes back, like the German Expressionists, to James Ensor, the Belgian, but has in him the spirit of a Frenchman — with his Ensor he mingles Cézanne, Daumier, Degas and Manet, seasoning it all with a little Cubism of the Leger brand, with maybe a dash of Modigliani. But out of it all, there is beginning to emerge something that looks authentically like "Gromaire."

Another youngster is Yves Alix, who hasn't quite found himself. Derain and the Post-Cubist Picasso seem to fill pretty largely his vision, but it's Derain and Picasso not yet properly assimilated.

The Cubist Survage, out of Russia, has developed an extraordinary surface loveliness, taming the wild jumble of Cubism, and bringing it into the æsthetic comprehension of the masses. He displays little of structural profundity in either his Cubistic canvases or his naturalistic studies of fisher-women, derived from Picasso.

A more authentic derivative of Cubism is Andre Lhote, writer and instructor, as well as painter, whose atelier is one of the most popular in Paris, and who is instructing his students how to combine what the Cubists have learned with what the Napoleonic David and his disciple Ingres practised. Lhote himself has displayed great skill in compounding the two in his own work.

Of late, Hyper-Realism has been somewhat eagerly watched by critics on the lookout for something new and worthy to succeed the near-defunct Cubism.

Hyper-Realism is a revolt from the more or less mathematical precision of Cubism — a new ideal romanticism transcending reality, and, as working out, being rather close of kin to "Dadaism". Indeed, the veteran "Dadaist" Klee has been caught as a stowaway in the ranks.

But the movement, if it ever amounts to much, will owe its prestige to Joan Miro, a Catalonian. Miro's "pictures" are sometimes little more than a few wiggly lines, running up and down his canvas or crossways, but somehow they linger in memory — a memory that seems to have a dim recollection of broken surfaces, more or less mystically harmonizing. Sometimes he gets closer to pictorial realities, as in his "Dog Barking at the Moon", whose simple grotesquery loses, on acquaintance, its bizarre touch of comedy and becomes as seriously haunting as his abstractions.

Before Miro, the leader of the Hyper-Realists, was Giorgio de Chirico, born in Greece of Italian parentage, and brought up amid the ruins of both Greece and Italy. Chirico, however, was too intent upon interpreting ancient Roman warriors and gladiators and war horses and Greek heroes and maidens after a peculiar vision of his own to play around in an "ism", and so he abdicated leadership in favor of Miro.

Chirico is being rated by enthusiasts as one of the genuine contemporary geniuses. It is certain that his visualizations of old Rome have a zest that David's lacked.

Of

ALEXANDER
ARCHIPENKO
and the Sculptors

ALEXANDER ARCHIPENKO lives in a world of undulations. His expression is the female figure — nude. Like El Greco's, his forms are aflame — flaming upward.

Rodin introduced into sculpture a surface tingle of flesh that marble through the ages had not possessed — a heresy. Archipenko has gone farther. He has made his forms live, with an internal fire. Scan a show of his quickly. The striking impression is vitality. Everything is alive — eager, dynamic, flaming upward. That is the essence of his work, its flavor, the distinctive quality that counts.

Archipenko, more thrillingly than any sculptor of the times, exemplifies the new "Expressionism" as it applies to marble and bronze. That he is the greatest

ANDRE LHOTE   LES DAMES D'AVIGNON

living sculptor will not be universally admitted until Aristide Maillol is gathered to his fathers — and even then there will be partisans to argue in favor of Mestrovic, and Bourdelle, and Epstein, and probably Brancusi, and Lehmbruck, and Kolbe and Barlach. And then there is to be considered as contemporary the very brilliant Gaudier-Brzeska, the Polish-Frenchman, who, fighting with the army of his adopted homeland, England, was killed, a mere boy, early in the World War. He lived to do little, but that little was tremendous, and gave a great impetus to sculpture in the direction of Expressionism.

Archipenko, even now (1930) only forty-three, has been in the eye of the art world for eighteen years. He has been the subject of much critical discussion — most of which turns out ultimately to be wrong or partially wrong. Criticism seeks to classify — to pigeonhole. Archipenko, a volcano of creative genius, inevitably bursts the walls of his classification — splinters to fragments his niche so nicely prepared for him in the archives of the savants.

"Cubist" he has been called, and is so designated in the already formal histories of the modern art movements. "Cubist", however, he is not — any more than is Picasso, inventor of "Cubism". He has experimented in the geometrical technique of the most vital art movement of modern times, and has produced "Cubistic" sculpture without a peer.

[169]

But Archipenko has passed through the "Cubistic" experiment, emerging with a power of expression he could have acquired in no other way.

"The purely abstract", he told me, in his studio in New York — for Archipenko, like most Russian artists, has no home in his native land in this experimental stage of the Soviet regime —"is a delight to the artist and to the few who can appreciate what the artist is striving for. But it is a barrier between the artist and the world at large — a needless barrier. Anything that can be expressed abstractly is also capable of expression in the concrete. The abstract form of the human body, which once so fascinated us who were working in the Cubistic theory, can be clothed with flesh and blood without loss. The work I have done since Cubism has in it all that I acquired during that period."

Archipenko, through all his career, has been obsessed by the nude female body, and to him the center of interest is the torso. As early as 1910, he did a "Salome", with legs chopped off above the knees and without hands. The face is stony and expressionless. Yet the figure is on fire — the torso of a dancer, with all the rhythmic, sensuous grace that provoked the most terrible tragedy, except one, in Christian annals. Regnault's famous painting in the Metropolitan Museum, with all its flash of dark eyes and raven hair, naked feet and gaudy Oriental robes, is only clap-trap melodrama in comparison.

The female torso, nude, can express anything Archipenko has to say. Through even his Cubistic period, his expression centered there. If he did not eliminate heads altogether, he did odd and bizarre things with them, to the bewilderment ofttimes of his well-wishers — to the dismay of his classifiers — to the ridicule and anger of the generality. Sometimes he dwarfed the head to less than the dimensions of a hand or a foot or a breast. Sometimes he elaborated the structure above the shoulders — normally the neck and the head — into a flowing hood or helmet, with the face a concave blank, or even an empty space — a keyhole through the marble. Always he drove the startled gaze back to the center of interest — the torso. Always was the gaze electrified, even under the whip.

Of late, Archipenko has taken to painting, seriously. He has always dabbled with the brush as a recreation, with results usually commensurate with his deft use of chalk or charcoal. During the summer of 1925 at Woodstock, however, he applied to painting the active brain power he concentrates on his sculpture.

Again, as in sculpture, it is the female nude, and again the torso is the center of interest. Again, there is a glory of undulation — a flaming upward.

No painter, with the sole exception of Renoir, has so conveyed the feeling of female flesh — warm and magnetic. And Archipenko has done what Renoir did not choose to do. Renoir's nudes are alive, but passive.

They are magnificent female animals, contented, bovine. Archipenko's painted nudes throb — every nerve quivers — feverishly they flame upward, like the saints of El Greco — with less holy fire. Archipenko may be attaining here the ultimate expression which modern Russian painting, floundering bravely and amazingly about, has been striving for.

Though Archipenko may be wrong, in view of his accomplishments, in considering his paintings mere "recreation", they are still unquestionably a diversion, in his mind, from sculpture. It is in sculptural forms he prefers to think.

The fire of his marbles and bronzes, increasing rather than diminishing in intensity as he proceeds, is all the more remarkable as the expression of an emotional nature guided and directed by a keen, analytical mind — mathematical and mechanical.

He is the son of an inventor who was mechanical engineer at Kiev University, in Ukrania, and has inherited much of his father's talent for mathematics and his skill in the construction of mechanical devices. His father mapped out for him the career of an engineer, but by the time he was 16, Archipenko had grasped the relationship between mathematics and art, as exemplified in the genius of Leonardo da Vinci.

Mathematics, purest and most abstract of the sciences, is nearly universally considered in our day inimical to emotional expression — to painting, sculpture, music and poetry. The philosophers of old knew better. Their highest poetic conception, "the music of the spheres", was the white hot focus of the intellectually abstract and the emotionally sensuous. In our day, nobody has experienced the quintessence of poetry who has not learned to follow a comet hurtling through the universe on a parabolic curve. Einstein, whether or not he knows what an iambic pentameter can do alongside a hexameter in a Spencerian stanza, deserves rank with the great creative poets of all time.

Enthusiastic admirers of Archipenko would place him among the mythical dozen who grasp the Einstein theory — perhaps at the head of the list, since Archipenko is credited by them with applying the Einstein theory concretely to statuary — a tremendous feat, if so, seeing how vague and tenuously abstract is the theory.

Archipenko, replying to this suggestion, when brought to his attention, observed:

"My knowledge of science does not suffice to understand the Einstein theory in all its aspects, but its spiritual substance is clear to me. I am convinced that life refracted in the prisms of art opens vistas to us into otherwise inaccessible depths, and when I realized the wisdom of the Creator in the words of Einstein, it seemed to me that I knew all that — perhaps I had seen it in my dreams.

"I have a suspicion that the theory of relativity was

always hidden in art, but Einstein with his genius has made it concrete with words and units. I am convinced that, thanks to Einstein, one can speak of art as something concrete; I do not speak of works of art, but of the mysterious process of creation.

"I had never spoken to anyone of this clear awakening of reason and comprehension which the Einstein theory brought forth in me. My invention, *Peinture Changeante*, I owe to the theory of relativity. In spite of my silence on the subject, there are critics who sensed in my creations and the Einstein theory a mysterious and inexplicable analogy."

The *Peinture Changeante* is a fascinating machine, in his studio on Fifty-Seventh street, New York. The observer is shown a screen on which is painted a study in pure abstract form. Archipenko then presses an electric button, a rapid, purring buzz is heard, and the abstract form begins gradually to change, assuming concrete shape. In the course of three or four minutes, the transformation proceeds through most of the phases of the female body Archipenko has painted and chiseled, returning ultimately to the abstraction it set out from. The machine demonstrates conclusively that Archipenko's abstractions, however bizarre they may appear to the inexperienced eye, have all resulted from keen observation of the female form.

If Archipenko derives from Einstein — or from the common fund of philosophy from which Einstein also emerged — he has had inspiration, too, from the empyrean to which Bach hearkened when he evolved his mysterious chords — "music of the spheres?" It was an Italian critic who first sensed the Bach analogy. The mystery of this sculptor goes far deeper than marble and chisel.

In 1910, Archipenko created his armless, legless "Salome". Sixteen years later, he returned to the subject — this time to express another of its tragic phases. Now it is Salome's affection for John, which Oscar Wilde introduced into literature, to the astonishment and shock of Christendom.

The new work, radically different, is no less astounding than a dancer without legs. This time there are two heads — nothing more — the detached, living head of Salome woven into rhythmic pattern with the severed, lifeless head of John.

As this is written, Archipenko is still at work on this amazing composition. He has the form to his satisfaction, but he is experimenting with stains. This is to be a colored sculpture, combining modelling with paint, not after the style so much of his famous sculpto-paintings, once a profound sensation in the art world, as in the mood of his new vivid expression with the brush. This new art episode in the history of Salome gives promise of reaching, in Archipenko, a visual expression that Oscar Wilde conveyed so vividly through the medium of words, and Strauss through music.

[175]

Archipenko, profound emotionally and intellectually, is the fortunate possessor, too, of a skill that enables him to carry out his inspirations deftly and surely in marble or bronze or wood, or on canvas. In adroitness, he resembles Picasso.

Though much of his work is beyond the grasp of laymen — even of artists and connoisseurs — so expert is his technique, so flawless his taste, that he has forced into popular appreciation a series of nude female figures, elongated beyond nature, but so exquisitely rounded and so marvelously beautiful as pure form, that even the more obtuse are hypnotized into forgetting comparison with bodies of flesh and blood.

He has done here in a great way with form what Aubrey Beardsley did in a lesser way with line. Few lovers of art fail to grasp now what Beardsley was driving at. The far greater master of line, Matisse, is still a puzzle to the generality. Archipenko, as profound in sculpture as Matisse is in drawing, may beat the Frenchman to universal acceptance of his genius.

Archipenko is a Ukranian, born at Kiev in 1887. "I come of a people who have no art tradition", he says of himself. "My ancestors, the same as the Russians, availed themselves in the past of Byzantine and Oriental influences. I like Byzantine and Oriental art, in fact all that is of genius in every country and of all times, and my 'tradition' is found everywhere — in the genius of human creation. There is no nationality in

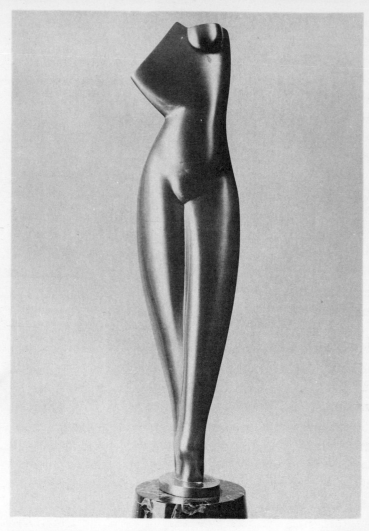

ALEXANDER ARCHIPENKO   TORSO

my creations. In that respect I am no more Ukranian than Chinese."

Archipenko's most vivid childhood impressions are of the great cathedral of Saint Sophia in his native city, with its ikons and its Byzantine frescoes. Leonid Andreyev was his literary god. The blood and slaughter of the revolution of 1905 was the tragic climax of his experiences in adolescence.

His early art studies were in the University of Kiev, where sculpture claimed his attention over painting. He went then to Moscow, where he remained for two years, and next to Paris, Mecca of artists the world over. He entered *l'Ecole des Beaux Arts,* but remained there only two weeks, finding the academic system tedious, irksome and puerile for his alert, creative mind and frenzied skill.

He haunted the Louvre, and from what he saw there of the sculpture of the Egyptians, the Assyrians and the Greeks before Phidias and Praxiteles, worked out his own salvation in his Montparnasse studio. He was only 20.

Rodin was the idol of the restless youth of Paris, but Archipenko felt the same sort of antipathy for the surface loveliness of the reigning master that Cézanne had felt for the evanescent beauty of the landscapes of the Impressionists.

In 1909, after he had been in Paris for about two years, Archipenko began to develop with assurance the individuality that was to bring him into sharp attention and to start the turmoil which has not ceased and will not cease as long as his creative, inventive powers remain feverishly active. He began to display with the Independents and in the Autumn Salon. His work was singled out for caustic comment and stormy controversy.

He remained in France — in Paris and Nice — until 1919, and then he set out on an extensive tour of the European capitals, exhibiting his work. He tarried for a time in Berlin. In 1923, he came to New York, where he opened a school on the order of the ones he had conducted in Paris and Berlin. His intention is to make America his home.

Alexander Archipenko, at forty-three, is already a leader among contemporary sculptors, and undoubtedly certain of a niche through the ages. Of his rivals for first honors since Rodin, the Frenchmen Maillol and Bourdelle were famous when Archipenko was born. The Serbian, Ivan Mestrovic, and the English-American Jew, Jacob Epstein, are more nearly his own age. Archipenko yields to none of them in the compound of intellect, emotion and skill, which spells genius.

More significant: Archipenko in each successive work gives evidence of growth — of a vitality vividly alive, like Picasso's. No matter how great the things he has done, there is always promise of something greater. Of his rivals, only Epstein shows this tendency. The fire of Archipenko's genius that flames upward in his female nudes is burning at white heat.

Brancusi, the hero of the burlesque battle over what is art and what isn't, fought out in the New York Customs House — as has been before related — has experimented, like Archipenko, in the abstract — but with one vital difference. If Archipenko is the sculptor-poet of the tapering marble flame, Brancusi demonstrates the triumph of the egg. It is from the oval he proceeds in the building of his abstract fantasies.

Maillol, who was born in 1861, was inducted into "Modernism" by Gauguin, and was well on the road toward the working out of his own salvation before the craze for the "abstract" hit the art world of Paris. Maillol kept stolidly on his way. He "distorted", but it was after the fashion of Gauguin and Cézanne and Renoir, always retaining the natural aspect of things.

Maillol, in his early manifestations, was contemporary with Rodin, but his expression was at variance with the master genius of the period, in some such measure as Cézanne differs from Monet. Rodin was hypnotized by the theory of surface loveliness the Impressionists in painting were preaching. Maillol leaned, like Cézanne, to the eternal solidity of things.

(It would be a mistake, however, to judge Rodin only an Impressionist in sculpture. Things like his "Balzac" and his "Burghers of Calais" are genuinely in the Expressionistic manner. Rodin, Impressionist or not, is the most important sculptor since Michelangelo.)

Maillol started out to be a painter, but, through the influence of his idol, Gauguin — himself a modeller in clay and a wood-carver — found sculpture more to his liking. At first he did little figurines, which he exhibited in the Salon of 1896. In 1903, he submitted some larger sculptures, which came near rejection — the liberal-minded Rodin casting the deciding vote in his favor.

Maillol, like Archipenko, displays his genius through the female nude. But there is a vast difference — Maillol's women are solid and massive — stolid and still — not restlessly aflame. There is a theory among certain of the "Modernist" art philosophers that the art product should be in key with the material of its construction. Marble and bronze being heavy and still, the statute should be massive and stolid. Maillol lives up to his theory, though he probably doesn't consciously subscribe to it — Archipenko and Rodin violate it constantly.

Maillol's heavy nudes, like the heavy nudes of Renoir and Rubens, are of great beauty, and their marvelous structure — their "significant form"— are unsurpassed in marble, ancient or modern.

Bourdelle, who was born the same year as Maillol, might be styled a "decorator" in sculpture. He thinks of sculpture in terms of architecture — as an ornament, though structurally a part of some public building or monument. That was the psychology of Greek and Gothic sculptors. As a consequence, his pieces, when displayed as a unit in a museum, lose materially in force, and fail to measure up to their intrinsic greatness.

Mestrovic models or carves with a fervor that amounts almost to agony, patriotic or religious. For his themes, he goes down into the soul frenzies of his countrymen. His Temple of Kossovo pieces are as though some American of real genius might do Bunker Hill or the heroic exploits of the South that were attempted at Stone Mountain. His Christs are from the Byzantine Primitives, only on fire with a zeal less powerfully restrained. Mestrovic is a great sculptor, with a little too much melodrama in his makeup.

Epstein has the faculty of setting the world agog, a faculty statesmen like Roosevelt and William Jennings Bryan possessed. He has gone through all the phases of abstraction with flying colors. But, before abstraction began making much noise, he did a series of decorations for the British Medical Association building in London that drew down much wrath on what has since become his devoted head. All he did, however, was to forget the Elgin marbles, which every true Englishman knows and admires, and go back to Pre-Phidian Greeks for his models. A Cubistic Venus of his, in 1914, again caused London to rave and rage, and he was next powerfully in the lime-light with a Christ, in 1917, with enormous hands, and with Jewish

[181]

and Egyptian characteristics in features and pose. A more recent offence was his bird fountain, "Rima", erected in a public park as a memorial to the novelist Hudson.

Epstein must not be viewed, however, as a deliberate sensationalist. That he can arouse popular antagonism is a proof of something intensely human in his work, amid all that is abstract and bizarre. In every instance where he has been fiercely assailed, the work attacked has stood the acid test, and emerged as a real piece of art, not a trumped-up bit of sensationalism.

Epstein is thoroughly grounded in the fundamentals of sculpture. He knows the Chaldeans and the Egyptians, the Chinese, the primitive Greeks — Phidias, Michelangelo, Rodin, and Brancusi. A keen intelligence guides his emotional impulses.

Lehmbruck, Barlach and Kolbe are giving something of the same expression in stone the advanced German painters are conveying through brush on canvas. Lehmbruck's female nudes are elongated creatures, handsome, with lovely breasts. Barlach's people are squat, heavy peasants, with a decided touch of comedy. Kolbe strives for action, and attains it — dancers, both male and female, are a favorite theme with him.

The Russian, Seraphim Soudbinin, should not be overlooked. He may not be one of the great sculptors, but he displays an amazing faculty for getting into wood the exotic spirit of fair wicked creatures of old legend — Leda, for example, who flirted with the swan — that Swinburne gets into his poetry — a spirit lovely and tainted.

Then there is that other Russian, Osip Zadkine, a youngster, who has done a marvelous *Sainte Famille*, suggestive of Brancusi and Gaudier-Brzeska, but assimilated, and his own.

The On-Rushing
GERMAN
EXPRESSIONISM

GERMAN Expressionism is alleged by various of the art genealogists to be the offshoot of Cubism — just as was Futurism in Italy and Vorticism in England.

But the problem is not so simple as that. The liberation of the entire art world through the bold declaration of independence on the part of Picasso undoubtedly had its effect in stimulating and accelerating the growth of Expressionism, but its trend was already pretty well defined before that memorable autumn of 1908 when Picasso and Braque threw their challenge to the *Fauves*.

Emil Nolde was doing decidedly "Expressionistic" things before the dawn of the century, and Max Pechstein and Paul Klee were full-fledged "Expressionists" before Picasso hung up his geometrical nudes.

"Expressionism", by name, came out of Munich

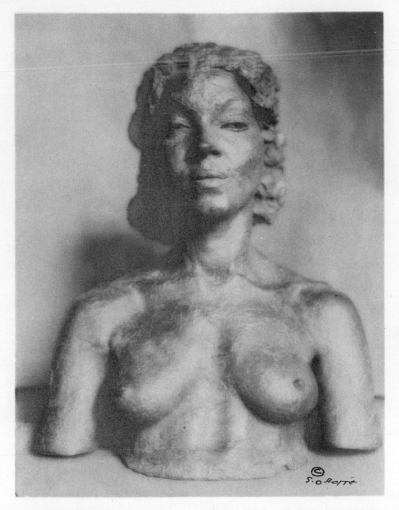

JACOB EPSTEIN   THE GIRL FROM SENEGAL

— a term invented when "isms" were running riot to cover the pictures and the philosophy of a group of artists gathered around the Russian Kandinsky. The Germans were Franz Marc, Auguste Macke, Heinrich Campendonk, the Baroness Werefkin and Gabriel Munter, and there was another Russian David Burliuk and an American of German extraction, Adolph Bloch.

"What cannot be defined is considered 'Expressionism' ", wrote the German critic Trog, a little testily, observing the activities of the group.

Kandinsky, however, seems to have had a rather clear idea of his own aims, and the aims (for the moment) of his associates. The Russian sought to develop in line and color certain abstract rhythms that would have some such appeal to the eye that music has to the ear.

An "art of spiritual harmony", he called it.

One such composition, painted in the winter of 1913-14, has attained a sort of immortality as being "prophetic" of the impending World War. When Kandinsky's attention was called late in the war years to traces of cannon and huge belchings of smoke, in his abstraction he replied that he had been conscious of "an immense conflict of forces in the spiritual world."

Kandinsky, however, was the only ideal "Expressionist", in the original meaning, since his associates had other aspirations in diverging directions, and the term became rapidly looser and looser until shortly it was

[185]

used to designate the whole German "Modern" movement, and then was extended to cover "Modernism" in general, irrespective of race and locality.

German Expressionism, in the sum total of its manifestations, has been traced to so many sources by the different thinkers who have gone beyond the careless theory of a Cubistic paternity as to indicate a much more complex psychology than any of the other "isms."

Dr. Oskar Pfister believes it goes back to Claude Monet, who begat (spiritually) Van Gogh, who begat Cézanne, who begat Matisse and Picasso, who begat (if biologically possible) the Cubists, the Futurists and the Expressionists.

All are certain Cézanne is somewhere near the origin, just as he is the fountainhead of all "Modernism", but he has been given strange associates.

For example, there is the German-Swiss professor Ferdinand Hodler, who seemed to me in the first edition of this book to be worthy of designation as a twin tap-root with Cézanne, but whose influence appears less and less important as more specimens of German Expressionism come under the eye.

Far more worthy, it seems to me, to share honors with Cézanne is the Belgian, James Ensor — emerging again, of late, as a major influence on the young radicals of Paris.

Ensor, Cézanne, Hodler, Picasso, Matisse, Van Gogh, even Claude Monet made their contributions undoubtedly, for the Germans are a race of thinkers and philosophers even in their art, and let nothing escape them.

But they took little more than the impulse even from Cézanne. The great German Expressionists are not lesser Cézannes, as, for example, is the Frenchman Derain. The Germans have had through the centuries a vigorous art impulse of their own, derived from Dürer and Cranach and their predecessors. When the Cézanne revolution started they modified this strain, just as Cézanne modified the French impulse out of Poussin and Chardin.

German Expressionism is, consequently, something radically different from French "Post-Impressionism". It is more violent, for one thing — cruder, less fastidious, more brutal — on the whole, more powerful and more rugged. It is not squeamish of "good taste", as French art always is, whatever its manifestations, nor does it observe the amenities of "morals".

It goes, too, more deeply into the heart of things, with the dogged perseverance of German philosophy. And when it sounds the depths it draws up whatever it finds there, no matter how muddy, how grimy of crude oil. The German Expressionists believe everything they find in the depths of their souls is material for their soul-expressive art, just as the German psychologists record everything they discover in the pages of their books.

This practice is both their strength and their weakness — reflected in the opinions of their own critics, the most profound art critics in the world, except — when they are dealing with their own art!

A critical genius like Julius Meier-Graefe will pass up the big things that are transpiring around him in Berlin to explain and theorize about French art.

A critic like W. Uhde, early friend of the early Picasso, and still eagerly on the lookout to detect new impulses in Paris, will complain bitterly of "all the irritating colors squeezed out of full tubes on to the canvas to fill in idiotically lacerated lines (Expressionism)" and assert: "All this painting by those who are emotionally dead, whose brains are in a state of convulsion, this painting which grows without either sun or sensibility in the shadow of ideas, of programs, of recipes, is but a 'local art', and remains foreign to all good Europeans, for whom love stands as the source of every worth-while act."

Dr. Pfister pondered deeply this resentment against the extreme Expressionists. He found that the Expressionist as artist "relies upon the sympathy of like-minded spectators. Tell me whose work among the Expressionists you are enjoying, and I will tell you who you are. For only he can understand the artist whose Unconscious speaks the same language as the artist's own Unconscious."

No wonder, if Dr. Pfister's theory is correct, German Expressionism has had so hard a time making its way not only beyond the borders of Germany but even into the great collections at home so rich in the paintings and sculptures of the French Moderns, including even (if not especially) the Cubism of Picasso.

But, just because the extremes of German Expressionism cannot be readily understood like the paintings of Cézanne, Matisse, even Picasso, Modigliani, Chagall, there is no good reason for dismissing it as insane, degenerate and of no artistic consequence, any more than there is reason to dismiss the obscure Kant.

"Only a fool", observed Dr. Pfister, "can disregard the deep seriousness, the very significant symptomatism, the absolutely justified and necessary longing for life to be found in Expressionism, this phenomenon of our times, this art-bolshevism spreading over the whole world of culture. . . . The Expressionists do not fall outside the framework of history, and of contemporary history, but they have shown themselves creative, bold to the point of self-sacrifice, and their inwardness borders on the incomprehensible, their originality makes the Philistines' hair stand on end. And for that reason Expressionism deserves the respect of all men, for it is a cry of distress, like a stream of lava forcing itself forward prompted by the soul's misery and a ravenous hunger after life."

So far the stream of lava has not disturbed us this side the Atlantic to any appreciable extent, and I am beginning, for one, to fear that it will not until we make of Expression a "cult"— a most distressing procedure, but sometimes necessary. Without an Ibsen "cult", for example, at the outset of his mission of dramatic reform, both English and American playwrights might still be following the Shakespearean model.

One enthusiastic believer in the German Expressionists — J. B. Neumann, art dealer, writer and dreamer — has lost a fortune trying to introduce the new Germans to New York. A few of the milder things have been sold, no more abstruse than the easier exercises of the French Cubists and *Fauves,* but America apparently will have no more of the distressing soul agonies of the great Expressionists than will Meier-Graefe and the annoyed Uhde.

E. Weyhe, another New York dealer, has brought over some of the easier things, too, with little better financial results.

In the 1926 Carnegie International at Pittsburgh there was shown a portrait of the actress Anita Berber (a favorite model with the Expressionists) by Otto Dix, done in lurid reds, revealing an almost nude body through flaming robes — all strangely distorted, startling and powerful. But, while Dix is reckoned at home one of the milder of the Expressionists, the picture was deemed too inflammatory for exhibition in the Art

Institute of Chicago, where the Birch-Bartlett collection of French Moderns hangs.

A beginning was made on the Pacific Coast during the Spring of 1927, when there were exhibited in Los Angeles and Portland works by Nolde, Kirchner, Klee, Kokoschka, Schmidt-Rotluff, Lehmbruck, Reichel and Heckel, of the purely German and Austrian, besides pictures by Feininger, originally American, and Jawlensky and Kandinsky, Russians.

Feininger was included in the 1929-30 show of "Paintings by Nineteen Living Americans" at the Museum of Modern Art, New York; a small group of Expressionists were a part of the International Water Color Show at the Art Institute of Chicago in the Spring of 1929; Kandinsky is well represented in the collection of the late Arthur Jerome Eddy, Chicago, no longer available to the public, and Bloch, now an instructor in a Kansas college, sometimes shows his work, but, for the most part, German Expressionism is an unknown and, apparently, an uncared-for quantity in America.

If and when it does come, there will be frightful headaches under "old hats" that will make the pains aroused by Fauvism and Cubism remembered as a pleasure.

Berlin and Munich are the principal centers of German art development, though there are half a dozen other cities, including Hanover, Dusseldorf and Mannheim, where ideas are apt to spring up spontaneously. Of late years the eyes of the world have been turned to the little city of Weimar, where there have been in progress some intensely interesting experiments in abstraction, looking toward a fusion of art and the machine — toward "Constructivism". Dutch and Russian artists have co-operated with men from Munich and Berlin. Some striking things evolved out of "Cubism" have resulted, but whether Weimar's aims are directed as strongly toward the fine arts as toward the applied does not yet appear. That is no particular worry of the Bauhaus, however. For cathedral building in Gothic times was intensely practical, but something fine resulted.

The German capitals, like Paris, have had their own art revolutions, and Munich boasts of a very startling and very successful counter-revolution, the "New Secession", whence sprang the acknowledged "Expressionistic" group.

Probably the most far-reaching of the influences out of Germany into the international art scene is that of Oskar Kokoschka, the Austrian, who is rated in Central Europe as on a par with Matisse and Picasso. Kokoschka's influence is beginning to be felt strongly in Paris, through the group that looks to Soutine as a leader — now that Modigliani is dead. Soutine himself derives more directly from Kokoschka than from Matisse, Cézanne and Daumier, to whom he has been

PAUL KLEE   A LITTLE FOOL IN A TRANCE

traced. Kokoschka goes ultimately, perhaps, to Cézanne, but in no such sense as Derain. He is an original
manifestation, like Picasso, also ultimately Cézannish.

Kokoschka has an outer ruggedness that strikes
the beholder at first glance so strongly that there is
instant suspicion that he is a trickster, a melodramatist.
However, as you gaze and gaze, and then return to gaze
some more, you discover he is as profound structurally
as he appears on the surface. He is an "Expressionist"
who has sounded the depths, discovered violence, and
brought it to the surface. The surface appearance of
crudity vanishes presently in the grasp of the general
ruggedness of his conception. "Adam and Eva", "Lot
and His Daughter", "Saul and David" are not likely
to go soon on Sunday school postcards, but their con-
templation might be serviceable in resuscitating an en-
feebled interest in stale legend. In certain other aspects,
Kokoschka re-creates Gauguin more brutally. But his
gnarled self-portrait may emerge ultimately as his master work, just as it is now his best known.

Perhaps better qualified for Biblical illustration —
or, rather, re-creation — is Emil Nolde, one of the older
of the "Expressionists", but no more lacking in the
fervor of "Modernism" than the aging sculptor,
Maillol. Nolde distorts faces almost to the semblance
of masks — not expressionless, but masks more strongly
indicative of character than the natural features. His
faces become grotesque caricatures, but without comedy.

— serious — and sometimes of a strange loveliness. Of this strange beauty are the personages of "Holy Night", Mary, Joseph and the Babe. He can be comic, though, when he wishes, and without losing strength — "King Solomon and His Wives", for example. Nolde is not as profound structurally as Kokoschka — he leans toward the flat surfaces of the decorative painters, of the breed of Gauguin.

Max Pechstein is impulsively or deliberately a "Primitive", not naive like Rousseau, but with a full knowledge of what he is doing, attempting to recreate the psychology of the savage. He misses the stolid passiveness Gauguin so matchlessly expressed, but his barbarians have a fascination of their own. That their energy is not accidental but deliberate is indicated by his recreation of a "primitive" stained-glass window, in which he makes the always passive Christ abundantly alive. Pechstein's soul is mischievous.

Mischief reaches the farthest point it has ever gone in art, however — a frontier beyond even the Satanic Felicien Rops — in the work of Georg Grosz. Grosz may be classified as a cartoonist or a caricaturist, but you'll have to stretch the meaning of the term to include also a very great artist — greater far than Cruikshank — greater than Hogarth.

The obscenities of Grosz will probably bar him perpetually from public exhibition, in his really significant aspects, in Anglo-Saxon lands. He is the most

ferocious satirist ever turned loose to scourge society
— teller of the most brutal truths, in the least polite
language that has ever been used in art. He uses the
method invented by the "Futurists", the X-Ray. A
society woman walking down the street, all be-decked
and be-feathered, is pictured that way — but Grosz
X-Rays her, too, and reveals her as of prostitute mind
and intent. His is a world of prostitutes and satyrs
among the generality of mankind, of boot-lickers
among politicians, of cringing dogs among men of af-
fairs — begging the pardon of the dogs.

Grosz, who has struggled along under both im-
perial and republican regimes in Germany, wielding a
scorpion lash through the periodical press, has spent a
good part of his time in jail. "Grosz's satire is a burning glass which reflects the bourgeois soul, consuming
it in flame", writes a critic introducing the plates in
an Italian monograph.

Grosz's cartoons are genuine works of art that will
endure. As a satirist he matches Goya. He is a powerful draftsman and a stinging colorist.

Karl Hofer made, in 1924, the experiment of
"jazzing up" Cézanne's "Card Players", and did an
astonishing job of it. In 1925 he undertook a still life
of skulls, human and animal, a true *Nature Morte,* it
would seem, but they are all laughing and having so
hilarious a time you wonder if they know they are
dead and bleaching out on the sandy desert. Whatever

Hofer does hits you with a force that makes you fear for your solar plexus. That's a habit of the "Expressionists"— a habit Hofer has intensified.

Paul Klee, a leader in the Dadaistic movement, scratches on a slate like a child — not the child of six, that Whistler accused Cézanne of being, nor the child of five, that Matisse sought to become, but the child of two or three. But out of the foolish scratchings there emerges something that is not childish babble — something a foreigner is trying to say to you in a jumble of his language and yours — something that makes its way vaguely into your consciousness, without your fully grasping its meaning. His is not the art of pure pattern, like the best of Cubism. Klee, like Grosz, is fundamentally a cartoonist. Grosz, despite his bizarre lines, planes and colors, never leaves you in doubt of what he is driving at. Klee is less explicit. You are led on to look for a point, where perhaps there isn't any. His work, nevertheless, has decided individuality and a hypnotic force.

Kandinsky, the Russian, is more abstract, but less abstruse. He is just a colorist — color violently and stormily in motion, like El Greco's clouds. You don't care what Kandinsky means — all you do is feel. The experience is not so unusual. What else is there to do when you look at the pattern of the starry sky on a clear night?

Franz Marc, like Marc Chagall, is the inventor of strange beasts that never were seen in heaven above, or on the earth beneath, or in the waters under the earth. His "Steer" of 1911 is famous wherever "Modern Art" is known. Marc distorts to his heart's content in the interest of "pattern." But he feels a right, also, like the Chinese, to give his own conception of the soul life of a cow or a dog — or even a nude woman. A certain dreamy loveliness is recognizable in Marc's work even by persons who are repelled by the "Expressionism" of men like Nolde, Pechstein or Otto Dix.

Marc Chagall, the Russian, whose development belongs largely in the atmosphere of German "Expressionism", we have already discussed in surveying Paris, his later art home.

There is a woman in the "Expressionistic" movement — as thoroughly in it as Berthe Morisot and Mary Cassatt were in the French "Impressionistic" development — Paula Modersohn-Becker of Dresden. She is a tamer Nolde. She has a rival in the wilder, but less talented Maria Uhden, who plays with the beasts of Franz Marc and Marc Chagall.

As with Paris, so with Germany — the new movement has developed a great number of artists who have emerged from the masses, but whose ultimate standing must be left for decision after "Expressionism" has run its course.

Among these are Friedrich Karl Gotsch, whose lyrics of the brothel are in a minor key when compared with Grosz's; Max Beckmann, past master in technique, but lacking, somehow, in fervor; George Schrimpf, with almost an Italian smoothness over his "primitives"; Heinrich Campendonk, inhabiting a world as unreal as Marc's; Willy Jaeckel, whose creatures move restlessly about, like the unhappy shades in the Greek Hades; Ludwig Meidner, a lesser Kokoschka, whose portraits have eyes blazing with something near insanity; Cesar Klein, with the placidity of the Sphinx; Heinrich Zille, somewhat better than an illustrator, looking at slum life with a coarser eye than Lautrec's, and recording brutally what he sees.

In Vienna, besides Kokoschka, are Gustav Klimt, decorative painter, with a sense of the luxurious; Egon Schiele, with as little illusion about women in general as Degas had about ballet girls, painting nudes with insulting frankness — women that stick in memory; F. A. Harta, who has been stricken by El Greco; Carry Hauser, Ernst Wagner and Franz Zulov, mystics, but each with his individuality, all obsessed, more or less, by religious legend; Robert Philippi, with his own peculiar style of elongating the female nude; Georg Ehrlich, dreamer; Otto Rudolf Schatz, man of the world and relentless realist, besides the very talented sculptors, Ambrosi, Hanak, and Josef Humplik — the latter undoubtedly destined for international importance.

ITALY
AND ENGLAND

ITALY, with Caravaggio, and England, with Constable and Turner, both contributed liberally to the original impulses toward "Modernism", but neither has done what might have been expected from art communities of their importance to keep the hot flames leaping.

Both tried. Italy threw into the bonfire something she invented termed "Futurism" and England tossed in "Vorticism", but both have been all but negligible in comparison with French — or Franco-Spanish — "Cubism" and German "Expressionism".

If Italy, moreover, supplied a mainspring for the new movement, in the far-off long-ago in the art of Caravaggio, she supplied at the very same period the Academism that secured a strangle-hold on art and held a vise-like grip until Courbet, Manet and Cézanne came to the rescue — the Academism that had its origin with the Carracci. England has been inimical in a different way — standing bullheadedly against progress, and even now as far behind the procession as America, if not farther.

Italy is earnestly endeavoring to come back into the international picture — to resume something of the glory that was hers during the Renaissance, but with all her striving — with all her background — she has produced so far only one world figure, Modigliani — and he was a Parisian.

Theoretically, Italy should "come back". The Italians take their art with the utmost seriousness, and no training is too long or too arduous to perfect themselves in the technique, without which "Modern" art or any other kind of art is superficial — worthless. They have not only the traditions — and the blood — of the great Renaissance masters as a vital part of their make-up, but they have Giotto and all the "Primitives" back of him, in whom art manifested itself with the rugged, spontaneous vitality that is the essence of "Modernism".

It may be as Alfeo Faggi told me — Faggi, the Woodstock sculptor, born and bred to manhood in Italy. It is Faggi's theory that the Italian artist is awed and repressed by the glory of his past. If he has a new inspiration and starts eagerly to create, he is apt to find, before the work is half finished, something done in a

OTTO DIX   THE ACTRESS, ANITA BERBER

similar vein by an Old Master. He looks at the master's work, despairs of ever being able to equal it, and thus is beaten. In another land, away from the glory — and the burden — of his traditions, he will go on with his inspiration with the eagerness of the start, with a fine chance, because of the skill he has acquired by long training, of doing something better than his fellows.

That may explain — partially, at least — Modigliani in Paris.

"Futurism", as we observed many pages back, is the Italian version of Parisian "Cubism". It may have failed to accomplish its program because it had none of the spontaneity of Picasso's invention, and was just a deliberate, intellectual attempt to "go wild".

The poet Marinetti was its originator and chief spokesman. He issued manifestos, and it was up to the artists to make visual his ideas. These ideas are largely vague, mystical junk, of no assured meaning in the reading, and the painters had a pretty hard time making them concrete on canvas.

At that, Giacomo Balla, Gino Severini, Carlo Carra and two or three others didn't do so badly. "Cubism" was static. The "Futurists" undertook to set it in motion. Balla did it with his "Dog in Leash", running along beside its mistress, with a hundred or so legs indicating the motion. This, and Severini's fantastic "Cafe", with everything that would transpire there during a period of twenty-four hours, all jumbled before

you, are probably the best pictures "Futurism" produced. Russolo's "Dynamism of an Auto", a series of
vortices indicating the progress of a motor car, has its
fascination. Carra's "Funeral of the Anarchist Galli"
has an emotional content that might be thought to rule
it out of a class where abstraction is so much of an
ideal. We are supposed to look "through" the picture,
not "at" it — and see the force that animates it. Carra's
masterpiece may be a little too "pictorial"— there is a
suggestion in it of the tossing, flame forms of El Greco.

"Futurism" was not of the genius of the Italian
art race, and it died of inanition, leaving little trace.
"Cubism", too, is passed, but the painters who went
through the Cubistic experiment have emerged with
something much stronger than what they had when
they went in — something profoundly structural. The
young Italian painters who have emerged from the "Fu-
turistic" experiment do not seem to have brought with
them anything particularly worth while.

Felice Casorati is perhaps the leader of this young
group that has come back to Naturalism. Casorati has
acquired the "Modern" habit of eliminating non-essen-
tials, and he has even brought into his painting some
relics of "Futurism", just as Lhote still retains certain
features of "Cubism". But Casorati, despite a great and
really strong surface beauty, does not exhibit the structural profundity of the French and German "Modernists". His is a superb skill, rendering what is doubtless

a sincere inspiration — but the sum total, despite its "Modernistic" cast, is no better than Tiepolo, in whose skilled hands Italian art decayed.

Ferruccio Ferrazzi, Primo Conti, Ubaldo Oppi, Guido Cadorin and Antonio Donghi, among the post-"Futurists", and Fortunato Deparo, who is doggedly persisting in "Futurism", just as Juan Gris is in "Cubism", all have a fine intellectual grasp of what "Modernism" is about, but in order to measure their significance, all you have to do is to hang them in the same gallery with a Modigliani. Modigliani is a world master. These others are just Italians of fine talent.

In England, the situation is even less thrilling. English "Vorticism" was of still slighter value than Italian "Futurism". Had Gaudier-Brzeska, youthful sculptor, not been struck down by a German bullet early in the World War, he might have justified "Vorticism" as a genius in the movement, even if he had not been a genuine product of its theories. For "Vorticism", like "Futurism", was a thing of manifestos. Ezra Pound was its chief literary spokesman, ably seconded by Wyndham Lewis, who also tried to give it visual substance. It, too, was a species of "Cubism", however much it railed against the Franco-Spanish manifestation of the geometrically abstract.

C. R. W. Nevinson, a youthful British painter of talent, went through the "Vortex" period just as

Casorati went through "Futurism", and emerged without anything worth talking about.

England's two prize "Modernists", Augustus John and Duncan Grant, have not dabbled to any appreciable extent in the wild heresies. At worst, they hark back to Cézanne, with a dash of Matisse. Both are admirable painters, but neither has the fervid elemental creative genius of the French and the Germans.

The Nash brothers, John and Paul; Ethelbert White, Robert Bevan, Henry Lamb, William P. Roberts and Sir C. J. Holmes have all produced some very respectable "Modernistic" things, nor must be overlooked the paintings and drawings by Roger Fry, who has done so much as a writer to make "Modern Art" comprehensible by Englishmen and Americans, nor those of Jan Gordon — illustrator, but better than an illustrator — who has also done yeoman service with the pen. Both are painters of high accomplishment, without stepping inside the borderland of genius. Of late, Mrs. Dod Procter has been accomplishing bravely. She is a Royal Academy pet, but even at that she shows much knowledge of Cézanne and Picasso — knowledge assimilated.

Besides, the best artist in England today isn't a "Modernist" at all. He is F. L. Griggs, most sensitive, most vitally emotional etcher of architectural subjects since Meryon. Great art, even though it be contemporary, isn't necessarily "Modern".

THE
AMERICAN
SCENE

MANIFESTATIONS of "Modernism" in America have been, for the most part, feeble and futile. As was the case with Impressionism, we have succeeded in producing a few very good imitations of the French, but we have not been able to assimilate Cézanne as the Germans have done.

Our American "Expressionism" is only French "Post-Impressionism" of a poorer quality, instead of being something distinctively American, as Kokoschka and Nolde are distinctively German. It was the same with our "Impressionism". George Inness, our best master in the method, while he had some considerable success in adapting the technique to American forests, American streams, American sunsets, was never anything more than a second-rate Monet.

No one of even the high talent of Inness has appeared so far to make "Expressionism" in America something genuinely worth while — something native. We take the French masters too literally. We paint Wisconsin as the disciples of Cézanne would paint Brittany. We paint the Indians around Taos as Cézanne would paint his neighbors in the rural town of Aix.

Out in the Taos colony are a number of artists who have mastered the French technique. But they haven't learned to apply it. They are trying to cut and fit the New Mexican deserts into the patterns of the French hills of Derain. The result is bad French painting that utterly misses the spirit of the vast American southwest.

The woefully benighted Indiana artists are doing something much better. Most of them have never heard of Matisse, and the exhibition of a nude by Modigliani would be the occasion for a special called meeting of the Ku Klux Klan. But every year they bring to their Hoosier Salon, held at the Marshall Field store in Chicago — Sears, Roebuck & Company haven't any space available — whole acres of Brown County forest trees, in spring, summer, autumn and winter garb — square miles of waving cornfields from the banks of the Wabash far away. They bring, that is, something distinctively of Indiana. One of these days a great genius may arise down there, patterned, maybe, along the lines of the late T. C. Steele, the best so far of the Indiana group — though he was no more cognizant of what

art is than Lew Wallace of what constitutes fiction —
pull all that "inspiration" together, and create something that will be great, big and American. Out in Taos,
unless they mend their ways, the more sophisticated
artists will still be painting bad French pictures.

Down in New Mexico, right under the noses of
artists who have not yet been keen enough to scent it,
is spread their salvation. Motifs are there from the
primitive men of the canyons — and from the Mayas
farther south — motifs as powerful as the African
sculpture utilized by Picasso — the idols of the Ta-
hitans, Gauguin found so valuable to his inspiration.
Under the blazing sun of the American tropics what
might not flourish, if there should appear the fervid
imagination of a Gauguin or the inventive genius of
a Picasso? Attempts so far to utilize Indian motifs have
resulted in "art" comparable with the fiction of James
Fenimore Cooper. The assimilation, when it comes,
must be a fusion in the fires of white-hot genius.

Then, there are the Sand Dunes along Lake Michigan, to which artists from various parts of America
flock every summer. Thousands of attempts are made
annually to entrap the mysterious spirit of the Dunes,
without success. When the painter of genuine genius
appears — the painter who has assimilated the skill of
the masters and then follows his own inspiration — the
Dunes may be found as simple to record as the famous
haystack Claude Monet painted a score of times.

[207]

America has been (1930) "Modern"-conscious for only seventeen years, of which at least five must be wiped out of consideration as impossible of fruition because of war and reconstruction. It is little wonder if we are in somewhat of a maze over the relative importance (if any) of our native artists of progressive tendencies.

Recent determined attempts to discover and isolate our "geniuses" have been productive of only one result that can be universally accepted — we have none! That is to say, we have not one artist of accomplishment so marked that he stands out like a Matisse or a Picasso in France, or a Kokoschka in Germany, or even an Augustus John in England.

One of those eager hopes that spring eternal was aroused melodramatically in 1928 by the importation of the German critic Julius Meier-Graefe, biographer of Van Gogh and Cézanne, and particularly the "discoverer" in 1906 of the long-neglected El Greco. The hope was that the great German, with a fresh eye, might look over our American pictures and detect the divine spark hidden from native critics, whose eyes are red from the smoke of our smouldering.

Meier-Graefe looked and saw — John Marin, water colorist! And so we all rejoiced when the great German got back to his study in Berlin and resumed work on his monumental book on Renoir.

America's "Modernism" began with the Armory

JAMES CHAPIN   ELLA MARVIN

show of 1913 — so far as not only the public but also any considerable number of artists were aware — and sixteen years later, in December, 1929, the newly established Museum of Modern Art in New York undertook to select "Nineteen Living Americans" whose paintings demonstrated most conclusively our place in the sun.

Protests, shouts of rage and ridicule arose when the list was announced from everybody except the nineteen, and the chances are that each of the nineteen wondered how the other eighteen ever made the grade.

Nevertheless, the catalogue of the Museum of Modern Art's exhibition of Paintings by Nineteen Living Americans, opening December 13, 1929, and closing January 13, 1930 — for better or for worse — will be an important source book for future historians of American art. The exhibition was the first attempt on a large and respectable scale to fix the status of "Modernism" in America.

The artists represented were, alphabetically: Charles E. Burchfield, Charles Demuth, Preston Dickinson, Lyonel Feininger, George Overbury "Pop" Hart, Edward Hopper, Bernard Karfiol, Rockwell Kent, Walt Kuhn, Yasuo Kuniyoshi, Ernest Lawson, John Marin, Kenneth Hayes Miller, Georgia O'Keeffe, Jules Pascin, John Sloan, Eugene Speicher, Maurice Sterne, and Max Weber.

The best that can be said for the list, perhaps, is

that every artist on it is worthy of a place on a dozen similar lists of nineteen that could be made up with little duplication and without going far beyond the little provincial circle of New York painters whom the Museum spotted as being the only possible "Americans".

So great was the furore that the magazine, *The Arts,* called for lists from its readers naming their choice of nineteen.

"The artist whose name appeared on the largest number of lists submitted", reports Forbes Watson, the editor, "is Eugene Speicher. John Sloan received the second largest vote, John Marin the third, and Charles Burchfield the fourth, with Edward Hopper, George Luks, Rockwell Kent, Bernard Karfiol, Kenneth Hayes Miller, Max Weber, Preston Dickinson, Charles Demuth and Walt Kuhn winning the next largest number of votes."

The balloting showed, in other words, that the yells of rage and ridicule were for the purpose of exercising the lungs of the yellers — that the protesters were inclined to accept the self-constituted authority of the Museum of Modern Art.

John Marin and Max Weber, on the Museum's 1929 list, had the honor twenty years before of inaugurating the "Modern" movement in America — four years before the famous Armory show. Sharing with them the honors of that far-off year were Marsden Hartley and Alfred Maurer, eligible, except for accidental overlooking, of appearing among the "Nineteen" of 1929.

The place, twenty years ago, in the case of all except Weber, was the famous "291", cradle of art liberty in America — Alfred Stieglitz's little Photo-Secession Gallery, 291 Fifth Avenue, New York. Drawings by Rodin were shown there in 1907, and etchings, drawings, water colors, lithographs and oil paintings by Matisse in April, 1908 — to the vast and overwhelming disgust of painters like Chase and Alexander.

In March, 1909, "John Marin and Alfred Maurer (the 'new' Maurer) were introduced", Stieglitz told Arthur Jerome Eddy. "The work of these Americans seemed to upset the equilibrium of the academicians even more than the 'jokes' of Rodin and Matisse. May, 1909, Marsden Hartley was introduced to the public for the first time."

Meanwhile in this period, Max Weber was showing (April 22 to May 8, 1909) at the Haas Gallery, a room in the basement of a picture-framing shop on Madison Avenue near Sixtieth Street, some queer pictures he had been making in Paris under the instruction of Matisse and friendly interest of the Douanier Rousseau. Holger Cahill, Weber's biographer, credits this Weber show with having "ushered in the most vivid and exciting of American art epochs."

However, the excitement in both the basement of

the picture-framing shop and the little studio of the rebellious Fifth Avenue photographer was kept within decent bounds. Only a few annoyed painters knew or cared — and a few puzzled art critics.

The squall burst in fury in the windy March days of 1913, first at the Armory at Twenty-Eighth Street and Lexington Avenue, New York, and later in the same month on the lake front of Chicago at the Art Institute.

Arthur B. Davies and Robert Henri were the chief instigators. Henri was a painter and an instructor full of vim for the gospel of realism as learned from Edouard Manet, while Davies, also a painter, but more of a man of leisure and a connoisseur, saw no good reason why America should be kept in the dark about what was going on in the art world just to spare the feelings of Chase, Alexander and Kenyon Cox in New York and Oliver Dennett Grover, Ralph Clarkson and Lorado Taft in Chicago.

Davies, Henri and some more progressive spirits banded together into an "Association of American Painters and Sculptors", whose purpose in organizing the now historical "International Exhibition of Modern Art" (as the Armory Show was officially called) is thus set forth by the suave President Davies in a preface to the catalogue:

"This is not an institution but an association. It is composed of persons of varying tastes and predilections, who are agreed on one thing — that the time has arrived for giving the public here the opportunity to see for themselves the results of new influences at work in other countries in an art way. In getting together the works of the European Moderns, the Society has embarked on no propaganda. It proposes to enter on no controversy with any institution. Its sole object is to put the paintings, sculptures, and so on, on exhibition so that the intelligent may judge for themselves by themselves. Of course controversies will arise, just as they have arisen under similar circumstances in France, Italy, Germany and England. But they will not be the result of any stand taken by this Association as such; on the other hand, we are perfectly willing to assume full responsibility for providing the opportunity to those who may take one side or the other. Any individual expression of opinion contrary to the above is at variance with the official resolution of this Association."

Then, this adroit orator, like Mark Antony, retired from the rostrum, and let the mischief he and his associates had set afoot take what course it would.

The personnel of this association is worthy of preservation as a roll of honor: Karl Anderson, George Bellows, D. Putnam Brinley, J. Mowbray-Clarke, Leon Dabo, Jo Davidson, Arthur B. Davies, Guy Pene Du Bois, Sherry E. Fry, William J. Glackens, Robert Henri, E. A. Kramer, Walt Kuhn, Ernest Lawson, Jonas Lie,

George B. Luks, Elmer L. MacRae, Jerome Myers, Frank N. Nankivell, Bruce Porter, Maurice Prendergast, John Sloan, Henry Fitch Taylor, Allen Tucker and Mahonri Young.

Many were far from "wild men" even in their day. A few, like Kuhn, Sloan and Young are still carrying on militantly as "Modernists", but most and particularly Davies and Henri, the leading spirits, are canonized.

Davies didn't miss his guess when he anticipated "controversies will arise". Nothing like the Armory Show had ever been experienced in America. We were aroused out of the lethargy that hitherto had characterized us in the presence of graphic art — though we could, on occasion, arouse ourselves to riot when the honor of an American actor assailed by a Britisher was at stake.

There was an uproar from the press in New York, followed by popular excitement such as sometimes attended art exhibitions in Paris. In Chicago the clamor was even noisier — at the finish of the show there was an uprising of students of the Institute's art school, and only the interference of the police prevented the hanging and burning in effigy of Henri Matisse, rechristened and visually reconstructed of ticking and straw as Henry Hair-Mattress.

In connection with the Chicago exhibition, it is amusing to note that simultaneously there was a show

[214]

in an adjoining gallery of paintings by Pauline Palmer, now as then a militant foe of "Modernism". Mrs. Palmer is no more reconciled in 1930 to Marcel Duchamp's "Nude Descending a Staircase", the loudest laugh of the Armory Show, than she was in those harrowing days of March and early April seventeen years ago.

New York and Chicago did not recover from the Armory Show after it had closed and was safe out of the country, but its insults to American intelligence seemed to grow more and more pronounced as the days and weeks sped by. This may have been largely due to the fact that the commercial galleries, trading on the excitement, were springing up, putting the wild, insane art on the market in competition with the sober respectable pictures of Mr. Chase, Mr. Alexander, Mr. Grover and Mrs. Palmer.

Not only was foreign art (particularly the "degenerate" French) being offered for sale and finding a few buyers, but young, ambitious Americans were turning from the venerable old gods they had been taught to worship in the time-honored ateliers of Paris and Munich and running after the strange, sinful new idols. Our native artists were beginning to turn out some very good surface imitations of the annoying stuff.

In the midst of the excitement, however, the world went to war, and in the roar of the iron cannon was lost the figurative rattle of the musketry of the art revolution.

During the war years it was somehow as dangerous to be an art radical as it was to take lessons in German, to drink beer or to swallow aspirin.

Only a few hardy souls carried on, among them Stieglitz, who showed African sculpture (basis of the "communistic" and "anarchistic" art of Picasso — the term "bolshevist" hadn't yet been invented) in the winter of the first war year, 1914, paintings and drawings by the dangerous Picasso and Braque in 1915, and recent work of the equally suspicious Picabia in the same year. It was almost like trying to circulate the Bill of Rights of the Federal Constitution — a procedure as perilous in the days when the world was war-mad as it is in this present era of National Prohibition.

Nor did Stieglitz neglect his Americans. In 1911 he had given Weber a show — Weber, by the way, was curiously neglected in the Armory furore. He was neither in the association, nor did he exhibit in the American section of the show.

Stieglitz had also stuck to Hartley and Marin and had brought out Arthur Dove and Walkowitz. During the war years, he exhibited work of these from time to time, and he also introduced, in 1916, Miss Georgia O'Keeffe, a South Carolina school teacher, destined to become most successful of the Stieglitz group, with the possible exception of Marin.

BERNARD KARFIOL   TORSO

With the passing of the war years and the equally feverish years of reconstruction, when A. Mitchell Palmer, his snoopers and the avid police were smelling out "reds" and subjecting them to mob violence and deportation, art gradually regained its courage, and toward the middle of the decade just past the art rebellion assumed almost the violence it had attained in the summer of 1914.

The rich began buying fine examples of Modern Art and exhibiting them, at first furtively, in the public museums on loans. Gradually the museums opened their doors a little wider to "gifts", and then some of them even got up the courage to make purchases.

The battle for Modernism gradually was won, so far as collecting is concerned — and the art schools are succumbing rapidly to the "Modernistic" influence, just as they surrendered around the dawn of the century to the "Impressionism" of Monet.

But we are becoming a nation of "Modernists" without masters. New York's Museum of Modern Art failed to locate our Matisse, our Picasso, our Modigliani, our Chagall, simply because he doesn't exist.

It may be because we have no "traditions"— and, of late years, we have gone as frantically in search of "traditions" as we have of "masters". Benjamin West, Gilbert Stuart, Thomas Sully and the rest have escaped so far, as being frankly British. But we have eyes on Blakelock, Ryder, Homer and (of late and with much enthusiasm) on Thomas Eakins as sources of American "motifs" on which we may construct our symphonies as the French do on Claude Lorrain and Chardin and the Germans on Durer and Cranach. It's a hope — but, we fear, a little desperate and forlorn. In none of them is quite the smell of the soil, or, quoting our friend James Chapin, "the pungent smell of manure".

Chapin, of the New York group and appearing on the prize list of *The Arts* "Nineteen", submitted by Forbes Watson as a sort of alternate to the list chosen by the Museum of Modern Art, has made a sincere and vigorous attempt at a pure American art in the new "Expressive" spirit — an attempt that at least approximates the results attained through "Impressionism" by Inness.

Chapin, in the enthusiasm of youth, devoted himself so religiously to Cézanne that he could almost duplicate the technique of his idol in depicting rural scenes of his native New Jersey. But gradually he discarded imitation and substituted assimilation — that is to say, he looked at New Jersey farms and farm folk with the eye of an American instead of a Frenchman, and he painted a series of canvases, now widely distributed through museums, that may, in time, be regarded as the epic of the American farm. They depict the farmer, and his wife, and his sons, and his daughters, and his hired men and hired girls, and his cows, and his pigs, and his horses, and his plows with a feeling for rusticity that matches anything the Barbizons have to offer, but without the soft glamor. Chapin's farm folks are hard folks, embittered by the brutality of toil.

The young Chapin's ambitious aim at something big in the way of Americanism may be contrasted with the veteran Max Weber's steady adherence to Cézanne. Weber is the more weighty painter, in 1930, but his soul is abroad with the big Frenchmen and the big Germans and not interested particularly in the American scene.

Weber, however, is regarded as "American" and is so — not by birth, being of Russian origin, but because his life since early childhood has belonged to America.

Two others of the official "Nineteen", however, are American only by courtesy, and belong in the list no more than does that other world figure, Alexander Archipenko, now an American citizen. They are Jules Pascin, a Bulgarian, affiliated with the Paris group, and Lyonel Feininger, born in New York, but whose education and art life are of Hamburg, Berlin and Weimar. If Pascin and Feininger be accepted as American, then we may point with pride, too, to Jacob Epstein, Jewish-American-English sculptor, as much of London as were our other Americans, Sargent and Whistler.

Sargent, however, always claimed militantly to be an American, and the Americanism of Whistler was flung so frequently into his aching teeth that American he was classed. Both, accordingly, should be noted briefly.

Sargent was our last painter of international note as a first-rater — a rating indignantly insisted upon by our British cousins, even though his native countrymen accept him at a lesser valuation.

Neither Sargent nor Whistler can be classed as "Modernists", as we understand the term since the Cézanne revolution, but both stem from Manet and the rebellion of 1863.

Whistler participated in the *Salon des Refusés*, but did not become identified with the "Impressionistic" movement in France. He made a distinct contribution to progress, however, by calling attention to Japanese prints — one of the vital influences in present developments. Just how great an artist Whistler is to be ultimately considered does not yet appear. He certainly is not in the front rank — with men, that is, like Cézanne and Van Gogh and Gauguin and Manet. He is still going largely on his own steam — he was a brilliant wit and clever writer — and on the steam of his shadow, Joseph Pennell.

Sargent is more easily disposed of. He is distinctly a minor artist. He caught a trick of Manet's, reduced it to formula, and cleaned up a fortune as a fashionable portrait painter. He was a sensation at the outset of his career in Paris in the early eighties, while the Impressionists still had power to excite the world.

Both Whistler and Sargent have long since ceased to be exciting. Though Sargent is only recently dead, he predates even Cézanne as a painter, and smiled like a well-bred gentleman at the vagaries and follies of Matisse and Picasso. And Whistler is before Sargent.

With the understanding, then, that American painters and sculptors have ceased to interest the outside world — even though Holland and Germany regard as the greatest living architect Frank Lloyd Wright, whom we can scarcely see for the dust the Mann act agents raise chasing him — let us proceed to examine further our roster of national and local notables.

The group Stieglitz brought out are still reckoned the "aristocrats". Georgia O'Keeffe has done the best work, perhaps, of any American, male or female, in the pure abstract. Miss O'Keeffe works with surfaces, rather than lines, surfaces vaguely defined, like gently drifted snow. Her pictures arouse some such emotion as is felt after a vaguely remembered dream. They do not fight you, as do the pictures of the belligerent Cubists — their effect is soft and soothing. If emotion be the soul of art, then Miss O'Keeffe's abstractions are tenuous art bodies sublimated nearly to the essence. It has been said of her work that it is purely feminine. It does not strike me as such, as Marie Laurencin's. It seems vaguely sexless — without any sex suggestion. Laurencin, like Sappho, is the quintessence of sex.

Arthur G. Dove, too, revels in the abstract, but without the irresponsible abandon of Georgia O'Keeffe. He can be sensed usually as definitely conscious of form.

John Marin is probably the best water colorist America has produced. His work seems to be exactly in key with his medium. There is clearly recognizable natural form in his landscapes, but the joy comes from the play of his color in pattern.

Alfred Maurer, a veteran in years, was once a "sound" academic painter. But catching a glimpse of what the "Modernists" were striving for, he had a vivid vision of his own, and began painting distorted women of hectic color and great black eyes. His was a spontaneous vision, a genuine impulse, something that originated in Maurer, and has become readily recognizable as his. He has been likened to Modigliani, but without sensitive reason. Their spirit is different. Modigliani's feminine creatures are feverish, burning with an internal fire. Maurer's are calm of pulse. Maurer, of late, has been doing flowers with an individuality almost as well defined as that of his women. Without being a first-rate genius, Alfred Maurer is one of the convincingly genuine and sincere American "Expressionists."

Another American artist, of a younger generation, who has developed a vision of women with a flavor of old-world authenticity, yet spontaneous and copying nobody, is Bernard Karfiol, born in 1886, who gives evidence of developing into international importance. His contribution to art is an adolescent female nude — a primitive creature of haunting beauty. Karfiol seems to have mastered the psychology of this nude, being able to vary her, as was Renoir, without losing either her identity or her dark charm.

George ("Pop") Hart is looming larger and larger in the American scene. He has the rough, shaggy spirit that Daumier brought into art, and looks at life with penetrating insight and comprehending humor. He is a globe trotter, with an avid curiosity as to what the Mexican Indians are doing away back in the mountains where there are no white men, and he carries this curiosity with him to Porto Rico and to the French market place in New Orleans. His visualized reports have a decided "wallop".

Walt Kuhn, most able and most resourceful of fighters for the recognition of American art abroad, is himself one of the best painters in the group upon whom he relies to back up his promises of merit worthy of international attention. Kuhn, however, is too wide awake to all that is transpiring, too eager to try everything, for his own good. At times he has done studies of young girls, drastically simplified, that have gone a long way toward demonstrating a real leadership. But, of late, he has muddled the effect by creating a series of huge semi-nude females from the theater dressing-rooms, symbolizing various things — but signifying much less than did his quiet little girls combing their hair.

Kuhn's associates in the American section of the *Exposition Trinationale* as staged in the Durand-Ruel Galleries, Paris, in 1925, were Paul Bartlett, Paul Burlin, Robert W. Chandler, Paul Daugherty, Arthur B. Davies, Jo Davidson, William G. Glackens, Herbert Haseltine, "Pop" Hart, Charles W. Hawthorne, Cecil Howard, E. W. Redfield, Charles Sheeler, Allan Tucker, Max Weber, and Gertrude Whitney.

The roster is a curious one. Hawthorne never did cause the Academies to lose sleep, and Arthur B. Davies long has ceased to do so. Glackens, like Davies, was responsible some years ago for many anxious moments, but he appears now as a late Impressionist with no more harm in him than Sargent. Paul Burlin spends a great part of his time in Paris, and his work is nothing more than a rather feeble echo of the Derain school of Cézanne. Walt Kuhn, "Pop" Hart and Max Weber supply what of "guts" there is in the exhibition, with the gentle Charles Sheeler doing his part with lovely things in exquisite taste.

There is also a group of American painters and sculptors resident in Paris who are "carrying on", and who were given a joint show in 1926 at the Durand-Ruel galleries.

Pascin, by courtesy, is a member of this group —

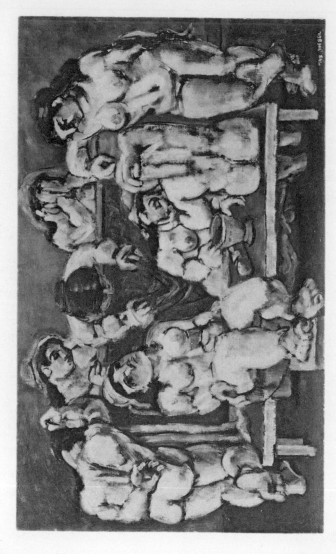

EIGHT FIGURES

MAX WEBER

he was in New York for a few months about the date
of the outbreak of the World War. Glackens, of the
Kuhn group, was also represented in the show, whose
other names are Oliver Chaffee, Henry C. Lee, Charles
H. Thorndike, Eugene P. Ullman, Clinton O'Callahan,
Gale Turnbull, Oscar Gieberich, Frederick C. Frieseke,
Harold M. English, John Storrs and Myron C. Nutting.

As in the Kuhn International, "good will" had a
lot to do in the making up of this show.

These attempts at storming the international cita-
dels, admirable as they are, are doomed to failure, under
present conditions, because — very frankly — America
has no more to show the world in the way of painting
and sculpture than it had to submit to the International
Exhibition of Modern Decorative and Industrial Art in
Paris in 1925, when everything not original and creative
was barred. The United States was the only great civi-
lized nation of the world excluded — and for the hu-
miliating reason that the few things we had were not
worth exhibiting.

Max Weber, Maurice Sterne and more especially
Albert Bloch have a touch of German "Expressionism"
in their make-up. They all start with Cézanne. Weber's
figures are heavy, but structurally are not quite heavy
enough — there are air pockets here and there. Sterne
concerns himself with line rather than with masses, dis-
torting somewhat as Hofer does, but with less violence.

[225]

Bloch occasionally goes all the way to Marc Chagall and Franz Marc, without the smashing effect.

Speaking of air pockets in the make-up of forms that look solid on the surface, Yasuo Kuniyoshi, a Japanese artist working with the New York group, has developed a very neat trick of filling huge female seminudes entirely with air, so that they look as though they should be anchored to the ground to keep from blowing away. Kuniyoshi is an exceedingly clever painter, with a whimsical trend of imagination that leads him to as bizarre wonderlands as Chagall's. His sense of drollery is usually at work when he has a brush in hand, but when he is doing still life, he exhibits an Oriental delicacy and skill that match his fellow-countryman's, Foujita, working in Paris.

Another delicate humorist in the younger New York group, but of a wholly different type, is Peggy Bacon, who very cleverly satirizes everything that is going on in the Bohemia around her — in the studio, in the "life class" at the art school, in the ball room of the artists, in the cottage in the country on vacation, at her dentist's, at her milliner's — anywhere where there is life. Unusually adroit as an artist, and with a sense of the ridiculous as keen as a razor edge, Peggy Bacon is producing classics of American comedy.

Alexander Brook, who is Peggy's husband, and a leader in a certain younger set in New York, is of Russian parentage, though born in America. He, too, has a sense of comedy, but holds it more strongly in leash. His comedy serves its best purpose in lighting up, from the interior, his creations, men and women, in a lightly Expressionistic vein.

Ernest Fiene, another of the younger painters, is decidedly a lyricist. His melodies in paint embrace the Hudson river scene and the Maine woods.

Harley Perkins, who is fighting the battle for "Modernism" in Boston as a newspaper art critic, is a water colorist of considerable skill, with a realization, like Marin's, that water is not oil and its products must be slighter. Cézanne illustrated the doctrine, and if he were not the greatest painter of modern times, he would still be its master water-colorist.

Wanda Gag, a young woman who has appeared recently in the New York scene, is a distortionist with a full realization of what distortion is for — that is, she doesn't distort to be different, but because she has something to say in that language. Her "Elevated Station" comes near being the last word on that phase of the traffic problem. Wanda Gag looks like an artist who will take off her hat and remain a long time.

Emile Ganso was a baker in New York, exhibiting now and then with the Independents, but spending most of his time making bread and pies. E. Weyhe, who, when he isn't selling books in the most picturesque art book store in America, is developing artists, took Ganso away from his ovens and set him to work painting. The resulting canvases are Cézanne brought into popular comprehension.

George Biddle, globe trotter, with Cuba and Paris as favorite resting places, turned of late his eyes on the Hudson long enough to see "Twenty-three Little Women" playing nude there, which he promptly lithographed. He had another vision of these same unclad playmates "Gathering Flowers on the Banks of the Hudson", and he completed a highly whimsical series with "Driving Home the Cows on the Banks of the Hudson". One of his nudes, later, imagined herself to be "Europa", and climbed astride a bull, while her companions looked on. Biddle, without being a master technician, is one of the most refreshing of our current art phenomena.

Annette Rosenshine has done some little distorted portraits in sculpture that come within the realms of both art and caricature.

Carl Sprinchorn, of Swedish extraction, is a dreamer of distorted personages and things, vividly colored.

Clivette, once a sensation of Greenwich Village, lays wild, flaming streaks of color on canvas, whence finally emerges a picture. He may have got the idea from Nolde, the German "Expressionist", though he displays none of the remarkable strength of Nolde.

The Zorachs, William and Marguerite, mingle "Cubism", "Dadaism" and "Futurism" with results that arrest the eye but do not hold it long. They have caught the surface trick without bothering about the depths.

George C. Ault, Vincent Canade, Stefan Hirsch, Niles Spencer and some others live in a world of geometry — not the world of the "Cubists", where planes overlapped and intersected until they became intricately jumbled — but where outward trappings of ornament and atmosphere disappear and only blocks remain. Each has his own vision — Ault's lines, for example, converge startlingly, and Hirsch's box-like boats have a dream quality.

Charles Demuth has also this habit of simplifying drastically, with poetic results similar to Sheeler's.

A. Walkowitz and Arnold Ronnebeck have reduced the New York skyscrapers and canyons they create to their lowest terms geometrically — performances rivalling those of the Russian and German "Constructivists".

Preston Dickinson belongs to the geometricians who have simplified in the direction of cubes, but he envelops everything with an atmospheric glamor that lends beauty sufficient to save him from anger and insult.

It is this glamor that the German "Expressionists" despise and that the French "Moderns" have succeeded in getting along without. It seems inherent in the American temperament — for Dickinson is only one of "most"— he carries it just a little farther than the others. American painting, like American plays and American novels, is seldom squeezed dry of melodrama.

Rockwell Kent, like Walter Pach and Walt Kuhn, is a vigorous fighter for "the cause", with tongue and pen. He has done some pleasingly expressive things, especially with wood blocks. There is a marked strain of mysticism in his work.

George Bellows, an American off-shoot of Manet — a better draftsman than Sargent, if not so good a painter — never attained to what is termed "Expressionism"; though his full masculine vigor — the vigor of a bull or a stallion — caused many uneasy qualms in the breasts of our "critics", who, for the most part, as we have already said, are spinsters (female and male). Bellows, in importance, belongs with Winslow Homer and George Inness.

The spirit of Bellows lives in his friend, Leon Kroll, who has pushed the Manet impulse a little farther in the direction of "Expressionism", and who is one of the soundest of contemporary American painters, if not an extreme "Modernist". Of this strain, too, is the lesser Edward Hopper.

The veteran Childe Hassam, once a sensation, never emerged from "Impressionism" into the clear — "Impressionism" of the Monet rather than the Manet type. Robert Henri, also, remains an "Impressionist", with stronger leanings toward Manet. The talented Ernest

Lawson belongs somewhere in this vague borderland, just back of the threshold of "Modernism".

John Sloan, who helped launch the Armory show, continued to sound the battle cry of freedom wherever his talents as militant leader were in demand. He organized and became the moving spirit of the New York Independents, whose determined onslaughts did much to reduce the once haughty academy to ruins. Sloan has accomplished well, too, as both painter and etcher. He is a mild Lautrec of New York's bohemia.

Charles Bateman, A. F. Levinson, Arnold Friedman, Maurice Becker, Peter Blume, Gerrit Hondius, the Soyers, the satirical illustrator Dehn — the list could be extended indefinitely of newer men who are lifting their heads a little above the throng, but the danger already has been one of inclusion in American "Expressionism", instead of exclusion. The demonstration in America has not been remarkable. Maybe it isn't in our temperament — maybe we must have a certain mixture of sentimentality — molasses and "goo"— to make our art palatable.

Though the Armory show excited Chicago to even more spectacular furies than it did New York, Chicago settled more comfortably back, eventually, into the bed of academism. With all its reputation for gun-play and gangsterism, Chicago observes better the traditions and the amenities.

But there is a very particular reason why "Modernism" hasn't produced on the lake front its quota of "Modernists" to compare with New York's. For, while it wouldn't be particularly hard to choose from the Chicago colonies "Nineteen Living Americans" to match the rather sorry Nineteen the Museum of Modern Art assembled in New York, still one such group of Nineteen would pretty well exhaust the Chicago panel, while in New York, as we have said, something like a dozen groups of a dead-level Nineteen could be assembled, so lacking in individual inspiration and direction are our Americans.

The reason for the comparative quiet of Chicago is that it is still living in "a glorious art tradition!" The "tradition" is none other than that, in 1893, there was assembled in Jackson Park in connection with the World's Fair the greatest art exhibition ever held in America — or that can ever be held! The sad part of this "tradition" is that nine out of every ten Chicagoans imbibed that idea with their mother's milk. It will take another World's Fair and another "greatest art exhibition ever held in America" to knock the 1893 tradition out of their heads — and that World's Fair will have to be held in Chicago! Chicagoans are that way — God help 'em!

Consequently, a "Modernist" in Chicago art circles has about as much chance as an Englishman in Mayor Thompson's cabinet.

Heading a Chicago list of "Nineteen", and proving

GEORGES ROUAULT   CIRCUS WOMAN

conclusively the smug provincialism of the Museum of Modern Art in finding all its worthy living Americans living in New York, is Salcia Bahnc, a young woman of creative vision, a thorough "Expressionist" in her impulses — one of a small group of "Modernists" who feel genuinely the urge of the new spirit in art — the spur to wild and free expression, unfettered by inhibitions.

From an aristocratic and wealthy home in Poland, Salcia Bahnc was brought, as a child, into the poverty of the New York Ghetto, where she was reared. She is of the family of Van Ast, which, for generations, has given artists to the world.

In her early stages as an artist she acquired a sound and sure technique, almost medieval in its profundity and simplicity. A portrait of herself on silk challenges the masters among the "primitives." Later she turned to Old Testament subjects on a giant scale — "The Shulamite", "Lot's Daughters", "Judith" — as "modern" and vivid pictorially as Swinburne is poetically. In this period, too, she did some remarkable portraits, particularly of Inez Cunningham and Katherine Davis, Chicago newspaper writers. She abandoned the "grand period" then to work on smaller canvases, principally female nudes, with results unsurpassed by American rivals.

The generalissimo of Chicago radicals is Rudolph Weisenborn, commander of the rebel forces from the time of the Armory show until recently when he refused re-election as head of the No-Jury Society, patterned along lines of Sloan's New York Independents, to devote more time to his painting. Weisenborn derived much of his early inspiration from the visual vortices of the English Vorticists, and added some violent colors of his own. He did some striking portraits in this fashion, the features emerging from stormy backgrounds of lines and planes. He was a thinker, primarily, carefully calculating his effects. After retiring from active battle for "the cause", however, he let his emotions have fuller sway in paint, and his later pictures rap as violently at the heart as on the head.

Weisenborn's unofficial instructor was the Pole, Szukalski, almost a legendary figure now in the Chicago colonies, though he was born as late as 1895. He was of such precocity as to be the chief disturbing figure in Chicago art during the World War. His was an astonishing skill and boldness of line, directed by a feverish spirit wise beyond his years. Painter and sculptor with equal facility, he was hailed as a "genius"— but time has seemingly proved his achievements were little more than of the "youthful phenomenon" type. He wrote, too — wild, rebel things — full of sound and fury — signifying nothing. He returned ultimately to Paris, and then to his native Poland — and apparently to obscurity.

Another of the early Chicago rebels is Carl

Hoeckner, who spent his genius on one remarkable painting, "The Homecoming", having in it all the horror and pity of War. Helen West Heller, also of the veterans, demonstrates an extraordinary talent in her woodblocks, nationally known.

Ramon Shiva, a Spaniard by birth, possesses a warm color sense above anybody in the American scene, comparable even with Renoir's. He has come into a strong "Expressionism" out of a rainbow "Impressionism" resembling LeSidaner's. Female nudes — particularly Negroes — are his strongest achievement, though he has studied Chicago's vistas with some astonishing blendings of drastic lines and rich color harmonies.

Rifka Angel is a Russian girl whose first contact with art in New York was, like Suzanne Valadon's, as a model. She learned to paint watching artists catch her difficult dance poses. Of brilliant mind, her emotional impulses are yet naïve, and her little canvases, which she executes rapidly, are playfully sophisticated. She is her own best model, as is the habit of women painters — and her range, without blotting out recognizable features, is from Cranach to the Chinese, through Chagall, Modigliani or whoever happens to be filling her fancy at the time. She imitates, but always as an interpreter, with a slightly humorous touch, and never as a copyist. She studied for a time in the academy at Moscow under the Bolshevik regime.

Todros Geller, profound student of Jewish art

through the centuries, and wanderer in the Ghettos of America, Europe and his ancestral Palestine, is producing of late some exceptional woodcuts, utilizing with intelligence and emotion many purely racial motifs. He envelops his canvases, too, with the racial atmosphere.

In A. L. Pollack, a Jewish clothing salesman in his late fifties, Chicago unearthed a genuine "primitive", crude and uneven in his work, but, when at his best, a match for any of the Europeans painting from untutored impulse, except Rousseau. His talent has a range of versatility extending from a "Crucifixion" with the railing thief instead of Christ as the central figure, to "Stockyards", catching for the first time we have noted in paint the weird spirit of that tremendous institution of necessary slaughter.

Emil Armin is another "primitive" in impulses, though sophisticated and intelligent in guiding his instincts to paint and carve. His work resembles somewhat the peasant art of Middle Europe, with American motifs.

The late Anthony Angarola attained national prominence with pictures structurally sound after the ways of the academy, illumined with a zest of spirit drawn from the "Futurism" of his ancestral Italy.

The Baer Brothers, Martin and George, associating in Paris with the Modigliani group, and applying to the natives of North Africa on the border of the Sahara motifs derived from both Cranach and El Greco, have achieved distinction in Paris as well as Chicago, and are represented in some of the more important collections, American and French.

Paul A. Florian attained meteoric prominence with a sensational canvas, "Two Nudes", somewhat in the spirit of Alastair. Florian, wealthy head of an advertising concern, then rested on his oars and called it a day in his art life.

Frances Foy does still life studies of flowers of rare loveliness, yielding to neither Sheeler nor Demuth of the eastern group. Her husband, Gustaf O. Dalstrom, head of No-Jury after Weisenborn's retirement, likewise avoids the "cult of the ugly" in his paintings.

In contrast, George Josimovich emerged from a drastic Cubism to do flaming, terrifying nudes, technically expert.

But we must be near exhausting the Chicago "Nineteen". There remain to be mentioned the Biesels, Charles and Fred and Fred's wife, Frances Strain, a trio of good painters and good rebel leaders; the Neebes, Louis Alexander and Minnie H., also valiant fighters for a winning cause; Tud Kempf, skilled carver of grotesques in wood, and his painter brother Tom; William S. Schwartz, overly melodramatic in his highly colored paintings, but finding himself in his lithographs; Ethel Spears and Helena Stevens, playful and whimsical, rivaling at times Peggy Bacon; Gregory Orloff, with a touch of Russian radicalism; H. N. Erffa, a

young German baron, idolizing Paul Klee and taking a
Klee impulse with him to Harvard; Katherine Dudley,
catching very successfully of late the spirit of newly-
rich aristocratic young Negro girls; Mrs. B. Hermont-
Schnee, a pupil for a time of Chagall's, and with a
touch of her own; Flora Schofield, trained in the
ateliers of Paris; Emil J. Grumieau, Beatrice Levy,
Ralph Erbaugh — somebody say when to stop.

In sculpture, Chicago claims Alfeo Faggi, now of
Woodstock and born in Italy, but who first made his
mark while a citizen of the summer resort on Lake
Michigan. Faggi's most famous works, too, are to be
seen in Chicago — a Pieta and Stations of the Cross set
in the very modern Church of St. Thomas the Apostle,
for a time a scandal in conservative Catholic circles.
Faggi has recaptured much of the religious zeal of the
Italian "Primitives", and his Stations are the best "Modernistic" work in the religious strain that America has
had in sculpture. Faggi, also, has done a remarkable creative work with a purely American theme — a figure
of the poet Walt Whitman in the nude.

John Storrs, who divides his time between Chicago
and Paris, is known perhaps better in his French home
than his American as a sculptor of highly progressive
tendencies. Of late, however, Chicago has begun to like
his drastic simplifications, and is to have in public buildings some of Storrs's creations. Storrs sees sculpture in
relationship with architecture, and even his smaller ab-

stractions have an architectural spirit, and may be regarded as a sort of simplification and rationalization of Cubism. They are of strength and beauty and easily comprehensible. Storrs seems to have no ambition to mystify. Portrait and figure studies are executed with taste and simplicity.

The late Tennessee Mitchell Anderson won national attention with her sculptured caricatures, culminating in a nude she called "Promenade", but irreverently nicknamed "The Pope's Flapper". The figure, about half life-size, was suggested to Mrs. Anderson's quaint sense of the comic by a newspaper report of the annoyance of grave churchmen over the growing nakedness of modern girls. The gowns had become so flimsy, it was alleged, the flapper might as well walk down the street with nothing on except a hat, a pair of gloves and a pair of shoes. Mrs. Anderson took the suggestion literally. The sensation caused by "Promenade" in both Chicago and New York was intensified by a report that the sculptor had taken for model a Chicago society woman immensely rich.

Though Chicago's "Expressionism" has not enjoyed the publicity, so far, that has fallen to the lot of New York's — since dealers have been more cautious on the lake front than along the Hudson in taking up new artists and exploiting them — Chicago's accomplishments, at the hands of a few artists, have been just as important, and Chicago has the better outlook for the future.

For there is nothing "set" in Chicago — nothing running in well-oiled grooves, as is unfortunately the case in New York. A number of the once-promising "Expressionists" on the Atlantic seaboard have arrived at a "pattern"— have reduced their accomplishments, unimportant as they are in the international eye, to a formula — repeating themselves over and over, as Corot used to do in the instance of his forest trees, and as Vlaminck unfortunately does now, having found his highly-colored landscapes salable.

More lamentable still, our Eastern artists, not content with an individual formula, have shown a willingness, of late, to fall into a broader general formula evolved by the particular commercial gallery with which they happen to be affiliated. It seems some of the New York gallery proprietors have definite ideas of what art should be like to be salable from their particular galery, and we have noted in more than one instance a fresh talent gradually succumbing to the "patina" favored by the dealer who happens to have corraled that talent. A "group show" in one or the other of these galleries is apt to exhibit a striking surface similarity between artists once widely divergent in impulsive aims. So far, that canker has not begun to eat into Chicago "Modernism".

Appreciation of "Modernism" in America has been

GIORGIO DE CHIRICO   NUS ANTIQUES

spreading like wild-fire of late, even to the smaller cities and towns — though the "die-hards" are still in the majority. The aims and accomplishments of the new artists are not a mystery to the young men and women coming out of the colleges. These youngsters regard with a pitying eye the "critics", museum lecturers, and prominent members of art clubs consulted by newspaper reporters, when they read or hear the stupid condemnation of features of art so easily grasped and appreciated by the alert minds of this wonder age. The "old hats" might as well be riding around in buggies instead of new-fangled automobiles — or condemning aviators as irreverent, flying in the face of Providence. Trying to stem the tide of the new art is like Tennessee's gallant fight against Darwinism.

Dr. A. C. Barnes, of Merion, Pa., who has the finest collection of "Modern" art in America, if not the best private collection of the new things in the world, has been largely responsible for the spread of this knowledge through the universities.

A notable liberalizing influence in Chicago and the Middle West has been the hanging in the Art Institute of Chicago of the Birch-Bartlett collection, presented to the Museum by Frederic Clay Bartlett, a millionaire artist, as a memorial to his wife, Helen Birch Bartlett, who helped him assemble it. The admittance of the Birch-Bartlett collection to the museum's galleries, after many timid hems and haws, gave vast moral support to other public museums throughout America, and was responsible for the scramble we are now witnessing for choice "Modern" things by nearly all the museums — pictures that once could be had for a song, but now are held at the price of a whole grand opera.

Another notable American collection, recently dispersed, was that of the late John Quinn, New York lawyer and bohemian, whose good fellowship with the artists was one of the comforting features of the early struggles of "Modernism" to establish itself on this continent. Nor must be forgotten the collection of the late Arthur Jerome Eddy, a wealthy business man of Chicago, who also encouraged the artists, and who wrote the most important pioneer book in their behalf published in America.

"ALL PROPAGANDA"?

THERE remains to be examined a charge against "Modern Art"—made maliciously by its enemies, and repeated anxiously under the breath by the more timid of its friends—that the vogue for Cézanne and his followers is the result of the unscrupulous exploitation by dealers and hireling critics, intent on making money for themselves.

F. W. Ruckstull, whom we have quoted before— the master condenser of all the venom that has been invented to poison the modern movement—thus expresses this charge:

"There has lately been given another proof of the truth of Tolstoi's remark that: whenever an artist invents a new fad in art, he, or his backers, soon trot out a new 'aesthetic theory' or 'principle'—to justify that fad!

"This has often been done, by a Paris clique of cynical propagandists of degenerate modernistic art:

[243]

artists, dealers, and their hired critics, all engaged in the festive game of unloading their art-trash — in which they only speculate — on the undiscriminating morons of the world, especially on those in America.

"But the most vicious and reprehensible trick of all, is the recent re-launching of the aesthetic 'gold brick' called:

" 'The Beauty of the Ugly.'

"This has been, and is a dangerous, subversive aberration; all the more so since it has now been imported into America, by the foxy foreign art dealers and their henchmen in this country: those blatant, charlatan 'art critics' who soil our leading newspapers with their cryptic lucubrations, and do it with such diabolic cunning that they catch the morons among our rich, and also many among our pretentious 'intelligentsia', in their vile campaign of unloading the modernistic art-junk on our people."

The shining example of "propaganda" that has been highly profitable is furnished by Ambroise Vollard, Paris art dealer and writer, who secured a great number of the paintings of Cézanne when they were all but going begging, who afterward wrote a biography of the painter, and who became rich when Cézanne caught on, and the skyrocketing of his art started.

Ruckstull (who, by the way, is no mere nobody, but was organizer of the National Sculpture Society of America, and first chief of sculpture of the St. Louis

World's Fair) pays his respects to this "sumptuous volume on Cézanne, by the Paris art-dealer, Ambroise
Vollard, written apparently to boost the prices of his
'collection' of Cézanne's works — in order to unload
them, at gigantic profits, on those American collectors
who have lost their sense of discrimination, and have
developed a weakness for succumbing to the weasel-
propaganda conducted by the masters of the art-world
today, the astute dealers in art — instead of going to
the artists direct, and buying what truly appeals to
them and emotions their own soul."

If it were only Ruckstull who felt that way, we
should let him continue to bay the moon unheeded, for,
despite his resounding honors, his utterances are so in-
temperate and actuated by such apparent malice as to
be negligible. But he represents a point of view — is the
vitriolic spokesman of a great mass of people who feel
the same way, if not quite so poignantly.

In his ravings he forgets such little points as the
fact it is not Americans who are the chief buyers of
the "degenerate moderns". Only a few of the important
Cézannes are owned in this country, and when the
great collection of the late John Quinn was dispersed
in New York a few months ago in settlement of his
estate, it was a matter of lamentable scandal how the
Paris dealers gobbled up the best works of all the modern
masters and took them back to Europe. The Germans
are heavy buyers of the modern French masters and so

are the Scandinavians. Americans run lamely behind
even the English, who are a bad second to the Conti-
nentals.

The charge against Vollard, however, has been
made by far better informed and more reasonable persons than Ruckstull. Even friends of "Modernism"
among the painters themselves have been known to
regard this episode with considerable cynicism. Without
Vollard, they have asserted, Cézanne would probably
be lying in neglect, perhaps forgotten. These friends do
not question the genius of Cézanne, but they question
the wisdom of the world — painters and art critics
included.

Admitting the truth of this gloomy view, it does
not need to depress us too much — for it only repeats
history. No great work of art — in any one of the seven
or the seventeen branches — has ever, in the annals of
the world, been known to make its way alone.

Without Ruskin, to cite a somewhat parallel case,
we would not have had Turner. Turner was already an
old man, living in comparative obscurity, his work
nearly finished, and neglected, and on its way to being
forgotten when the first volume of "Modern Painters"
appeared. The aging artist, who was not particularly
bright of intellect, only vaguely grasped himself what
his young admirer was driving at. Ruskin, however,
spoke so brilliantly, so incisively, so convincingly that
the rest of England understood — or thought it under-

stood — and Turner had thrust upon him the role of "great master".

It is true Ruskin was no dealer and he did not profit in dollars and cents by the rise of Turner into fame as did Vollard when Cézanne began to find favor. But to give Vollard credit for foisting on the world a charlatan who has changed the whole course of art history throughout the earth is to credit him with a miracle. Had not Cézanne been able to live up to Vollard's estimate of him, Vollard would have been discredited, just as Ruskin would have been laughed down as a critic had not Turner been able to meet his specification. Great art must have its spokesman, but once the spokesman is found, it must back up what he says.

Vollard's task, it may be, was harder, because his material interests laid him under a suspicion which Ruskin escaped. Vollard had the fortune, however, to have a far better cause, a far greater genius, than Ruskin.

A reading of Vollard's "Cézanne", which, fortunately, is available in English, will at once dispel in the mind of anyone free from prejudice the charges of servile self-seeking that have been brought against the author. It is one of the most vividly human biographies produced even in this age — the age when the greatest biographies of all time are being written. Vollard was genuinely interested in Cézanne the person and Cézanne the painter — not just in the canvases he had in his shop. Moreover, Vollard is the author of an almost equally thrilling volume on "Renoir", whom he did not "put across", and another on "Degas", that could have profited him little in the sale of paintings.

Vollard happens to be a very keen writer on art, with a human point of view that Ruskin lacked — you have to go back to the gossipy Vasari to match him in this respect. It is lucky for the world he was so well able to keep mere "propaganda" for Cézanne out of his biography, and anyone with a generous nature will rather rejoice that Vollard's early enthusiasm for the Master of Aix, when he was despised and rejected in other quarters, was at last financially rewarded.

Lamentable it is — but the truth cannot be denied — that, as we have said, no great work of art has ever been able to make its way without its literary spokes- man. This is so of literature, even, which would seem to be able to speak for itself.

Byron woke up to find himself famous, not because he had just written "Childe Harold", but because the Scotch reviewers had discovered it and given it a good notice.

The "Rubaiyat" was mussed over, for years, in the old book stalls until somebody discovered it and told the world about it.

The vogue of Homer is due to the "grammarians", and Shakespeare was decidedly a second-rater with every cheap English playwright revising and rewriting him, until the German critics stumbled onto him and told the English what they had. It was these German critics, by the way, in another generation, who discovered the French "moderns", particularly Picasso.

No actor ever becomes famous without newspaper plaudits — hence the army of well-paid press agents.

The Canadian Rockies, more sublime in grandeur than the Alps, suffer for lack of a literary spokesman of genius.

Emerson's superior cobbler, making shoes in the wilderness, may at last find a path beaten to his door, but he'll be an old man then, and get little joy out of selling his shoes. He'll be much happier if he'll get a bright newspaper reporter to give him a "Sunday story" about them, and more particularly about his picturesque woodland hut and what he eats for breakfast.

It is no cause for unique distress, therefore, that we have Cézanne largely because of Vollard. The whole situation is sad, but there's no particular reason for a special flood of tears over the Cézanne episode.

The Vollard story, however, has been a little exaggerated. Vollard paid "the sum of 80,000 or 90,000 francs" for his two hundred Cézannes, according to Theodore Duret. Cézanne's stock was already beginning to rise slightly in the world, when Vollard made his appearance. He was shrewd enough to appreciate the value of what others were sensing also. In other words, he did not buy a lot of unsalable junk and set out to sell it.

Before Vollard, there was another dealer interested — a dealer to whom Vollard pays generous tribute in his book — a dealer perpetually poor because of his devotion to young painters in whom he had faith shared by few of his customers. He was Père Tanguy, of whom Van Gogh, another of his clients, had left so expressive a portrait, and Emile Bernard so touching a literary tribute.

Father Tanguy, as he became affectionately known in the bohemian circles of Paris, came to the city from the north of France about 1860, the period of the outbreak of the "art revolution". He was a color grinder, and, in peddling his own paints, came in contact with Monet, Renoir, Pissarro, Cézanne and the other youthful rebels, soon to be known as "Impressionists".

Tanguy had a strain of rebel blood in his own veins — so strong, indeed, that he joined the Communists in 1871, and got into trouble with the police. He survived, however, and after the close of the Franco-Prussian war opened a little shop, where he not only sold his colors, but exchanged them for paintings or bought pictures outright from struggling artists who needed the cash more.

In this way he acquired paintings by Cézanne that nobody else would buy — and paintings by Van Gogh, Gauguin, Renoir, Pissarro, and the rest. Father Tanguy was not particularly enthusiastic over their salability at a profit, but he was more than making a living with his colors, and he was willing to share his meager surplus with friends less fortunate, and take a chance.

Cézanne was his favorite — probably because Cézanne was the most berated of all the painters, not only by customers, but by his painter associates. Van Gogh was his second choice — the Dutchman's wild social theories found an echo in Père Tanguy's communistic breast.

Both painters, however, gradually made their way into the color merchant's art consciousness, and when dark days came near the end of his life, in the middle eighties, it was to their pictures he clung longest in the forced sale of his possessions. He died in want, and artist friends contributed canvases for an auction sale to relieve the poverty of his widow.

It was Père Tanguy who first made known Cézanne's paintings to Paris — and if Père Tanguy was an unscrupulous charlatan, unloading his vile, degenerate trash on morons to pile up tainted coin for himself, make the most of it. He is closer to the type of dealers who nurse new things in art to their detriment — impractical fools, from the business man's standpoint — than is Vollard.

It was in Father Tanguy's shop that Cézanne's paintings were first discussed — a heated discussion, from the start, destined to grow loud and angry. It

was from Father Tanguy that the first collectors of
Cézanne bought works as "curios"— paintings that
would now bring fabulous sums from museums so
anxious for representative Cézannes.

These pictures, Père Tanguy sold according to size
— one size bringing so many francs, and a larger size
so many more. He was even prevailed upon to cut up
a few still life studies, and sell individual apples to
seekers of "souvenirs".

Cèzanne was pretty well known around Paris when
Vollard made his advent. Even the professional critics
were having their say, and some of the opinions were
not uncomplimentary. Vollard bought up everything
he could, and then brought the case of Cézanne for
trial before the jury of the world.

Theodore Duret, historian of the Impressionists,
and the writer who probably did more than anybody
else to make the revolution a dignified success in Paris,
was not unfriendly to Cézanne, but his god was Manet.
Duret, like Zola, missed the big significance of the
overwhelming genius of the group.

The charge that Cézanne's extraordinary renown
is the result of clever "propaganda" by dealers and paid
henchmen has been repeated in the cases of Matisse and
Picasso, and will continue to be repeated as long as
new men of genius arise with original, revolutionary
ideas.

"Propaganda" can accomplish wonders, but it cannot

AMEDEE MODIGLIANI   JEUNE FILLE

work miracles. "Modernism" has been in the world long enough to demonstrate it is no sensation of an hour. "Propaganda" could have created such a sensation, but it could never have sustained the phenomenon "Modern Art" has proven itself to be. The roots of the new art are in the age-old soil from which all great art has sprung. Cézanne, already, is taking his place with the Masters of all time.

INDEX

[255]

INDEX

[257]

INDEX

INDEX

ERRATA

page x PABLO PICASSO *for*
PAUL PICASSO

page xi SALCIA BAHNC: The Shulamite
COURTESY OF THE PAINTER *for*
SALCIA BAHNC: The Shulamite
IN THE GALLERY OF LIVING ART, NEW YORK UNIVERSITY

page xi JOAN MIRO: Dog Barking at the Moon
IN THE GALLERY OF LIVING ART, NEW YORK UNIVERSITY *for*
JOAN MIRO: Dog Barking at the Moon
COURTESY OF THE PAINTER